Contemporary Issues
in Mediation

Volume 1

Contemporary Issues
in Mediation

Volume 1

Dear Paul,

Thank you for your support!

Looking forward to a great working relationship. 15/08/17

Joel Lee & Marcus Lim

Singapore International Mediation Institute, Singapore

with Phua Jun Han

SINGAPORE INTERNATIONAL
MEDIATION INSTITUTE

World Scientific

Published by

World Scientific Publishing Co. Pte. Ltd.

5 Toh Tuck Link, Singapore 596224

USA office: 27 Warren Street, Suite 401-402, Hackensack, NJ 07601

UK office: 57 Shelton Street, Covent Garden, London WC2H 9HE

Library of Congress Cataloging-in-Publication Data

Names: Lee, Joel, editor. | Lim, Marcus, editor.

Title: Contemporary issues in mediation / Edited by Joel Lee
    (Singapore International Mediation Institute, Singapore),
    Marcus Lim (Singapore International Mediation Institute, Singapore).

Description: Hackensack, New Jersey : World Scientific, 2016.

Identifiers: LCCN 2016004240| ISBN 9789813108356 (hardcover : alk. paper) |
    ISBN 9789813108363 (pbk.)

Subjects: LCSH: Dispute resolution (Law) | Mediation. | Dispute resolution (Law)--Singapore. |
    Mediation--Singapore.

Classification: LCC K2390 .C667 2016 | DDC 347/.09--dc23

LC record available at http://lccn.loc.gov/2016004240

British Library Cataloguing-in-Publication Data

A catalogue record for this book is available from the British Library.

Desk Editor: Qi Xiao

Typeset by Stallion Press
Email: enquiries@stallionpress.com

Printed in Singapore

Contents

Foreword for the Series

By William Ury

A young man was hiking through the woods. He came to a clearing and sat on a rock to rest. As he ate his lunch, he noticed an old man moving through the clearing in a very deliberate way. The man would walk a specific number of steps, poke a hole in the ground with his walking stick, drop something in and then repeat the process. Curious, the young man approached the old man and asked him what he was doing.

The old man replied, "Well, I'm planting trees."

"But why?" the young man asked.

"When I was younger," the old man said, "this entire land was filled with trees. But over time, many trees had been cut down. I come here every day to plant trees."

Fascinated, the young man asked, "How long have you been doing this?"

"Forty years." was the matter of fact reply.

"Forty years!" exclaimed the young man.

"Yup," the old man replied. Gesturing to a grove of young trees in the distance, he said with some pride, "I planted those 10 years ago." The young man was incredulous. "That's great but these trees will take a long time to grow! And, if you will pardon me saying so, you may not live long enough to see the seeds you are planting today grow into trees!"

"This is true," said the old man "I have lived long enough to see some of the fruits of my labour. But the seeds I plant today are not for me, but for you."

It has now been just about 40 years since I had the privilege of embarking on the adventure of teaching and practicing in the field of negotiation and mediation. During that time, I have had the joy of learning from and working with many highly talented and skilled individuals in academia, law, business and diplomacy. In those early days, there was very little scholarly writing in this area. After all, the field was relatively new and viewed by many with caution, if not outright skepticism.

Over the years, I have been gratified to watch the field of mediation grow considerably. Today, practitioners, teachers and researchers can be found in every part of the world. The teaching, practice and scholarship of negotiation and mediation constitute a dynamic system in which each contributes to the others. New tools and frameworks have been developed as a result of research, taught to practitioners, and then tested and refined in the field, which in turn has informed further research. This interplay between theory and practice has been vital in developing new insights and methods.

Yet the field of negotiation and mediation is still young. As we look back on the progress, we might be satisfied with the seeds we have planted which have sprouted into trees. Yet, as the concepts and practices spread around the world, we have a responsibility to ensure that future generations will be able to build on all that has been achieved. We must continue to plant seeds, not for ourselves, but for those to come.

This is why this book project by the Singapore International Mediation Institute is such a timely endeavour worthy of support. It is said that a journey of a thousand miles begins with a single step. The Singapore International Mediation Institute is taking that first step to inspire the youth of today and encourage them to engage in scholarship about mediation. It provides them the platform and the opportunity to plant seeds for the benefit and enjoyment of future generations.

As the first of its kind in Singapore, I look forward to seeing this book series not only continue to flourish, but also to show the way forward through innovative and thought-provoking work.

And I take this opportunity to wish you much success in getting to yes!

William Ury
Co-founder, Harvard Negotiation Project
Co-author, *Getting to Yes*
31 May 2016

About the Editors

Joel Lee

 Joel Lee is an Associate Professor at the Faculty of Law, the National University of Singapore. Joel co-pioneered the teaching of Negotiation and Mediation in the Singapore Universities and has played a significant role in furthering the development of mediation in Singapore, not just in education but in practice. A graduate of Victoria University of Wellington and Harvard Law Schools, Joel is an affiliate partner with CMPartners (USA), and a principal mediator with and the Training Director of the Singapore Mediation Centre.

Joel is an adjudicator with the Financial Industry Disputes Resolution Centre and was a member of the International Mediation Institute's Independent Standards Commission and Intercultural Taskforce. He was also a key member of the Ministry of Law's Working Group on International Commercial Mediation. Joel is currently the founding Chair of the Board of the Singapore International Mediation Institute.

Joel has taught overseas at the University of Copenhagen (Denmark), University of Law, Economics and Science of Aix-Marseille (Aix-en-Provence France) and Anglia Law School (UK), and is the co-editor and co-author of the book *An Asian Perspective on Mediation* and the General Editor for the *Asian Journal on Mediation*. In 2011, Joel was awarded the Outstanding Educator Award which is the National University of Singapore's highest teaching award.

Marcus Lim

Marcus Lim is the Executive Director of the Singapore International Mediation Institute (SIMI). He also assists in running the Negotiation and Mediation Workshops at the Faculty of Law, the National University of Singapore. A graduate of the National University of Singapore from the prestigious Law and Business Double Degree program, he is also an Associate Mediator with the Singapore Mediation Centre.

Marcus is a volunteer mediator for the Small Claims Tribunal at the State Courts, as well as the Healthcare Mediator Panel under the MOHH Healthcare Mediation Scheme. Prior to joining SIMI, Marcus was an Associate with Rajah & Tann LLP's Competition and Technology, Media and Telecommunications Practice Group.

Marcus also has experience training staff and management of multinational corporations in financial, retail, real estate, IT, education and healthcare industries.

Editors' Note

Every book, like super heroes, has an origin story. This book, *Contemporary Issues in Mediation (Volume 1)*, is no exception (although no radioactive spiders were involved). It began with the editors of this book wondering why it was so difficult for their students in mediation to get published.

Was it because the pieces were not intellectual enough? Or was it perhaps in a field like mediation, the lack of practical and practice-based experience was the problem?

As the saying goes, "In Vino Veritas".[1] As the conversation and afternoon progressed, a number of truths emerged.

First, there is some truth that in a practice-based field, students simply do not have the experience (yet) to write about practice. However, and this is the second truth, one of the flaws of a practice-based field is that not enough thought is given to constructing coherent theories and frameworks for the purpose of training the next generation of practitioners and to guide practitioners through the grays (and years) of practice. In our experience, students bring fresh eyes, without the filters and biases that may have accumulated from practice. However, the third truth, and probably the key reason why it is so hard to get student pieces published, is that there is a bias — an intellectual snobbishness against student pieces. It is almost as if there is a presumption that if it is a student piece, it is not worthy of publication.

Of course, we acknowledge that these are generalizations which, by definition, cannot be and are probably not universally true. Yet by and large, this has been our experience. This is why we decided it was time to start this book series, *Contemporary Issues in Mediation*. It is premised on a vision that wisdom is not necessarily a function of age or experience and pieces that can meaningfully contribute to the development of the field

---

[1] "In Wine, Truth".

can come from students. *Contemporary Issues in Mediation* seeks to provide students the opportunity to showcase their work.

The pieces in this volume come from the top entries of the inaugural Singapore International Mediation Institute (SIMI) Annual Essay Competition.

The winning submission by NG Wan Qing explores the issue of power imbalance but through the lens of culture. Often we take the notion of power and the role of a mediator in the context of a power imbalance as an absolute given. Ng's work provides innovative nuance to this by examining it in the context of the Power Distance Index as well as against the interaction of Confucian values and the Individualism/Collectivism Index.

The submission that took second place is Valencia SOH's piece on the ethical obligations of a responsible mediation advocate. In it, she explores and assesses the various duties in the context of mediation.

Javier YEO's piece on the Facilitative and the Evaluative Divide deserves honourable mention. Yeo takes this age-old debate and critically examines the real differences between these two positions and provides a way to reconcile them.

The other seven pieces provide unique insights into a wide range of topics that we feel readers with an interest in mediation or even dispute resolution in general, will find thought-provoking and valuable.

This publication is the product of the efforts of many. We would like to take this opportunity to thank:

— Our better halves, Pearl and Li Jing, for their unending patience and understanding;
— Mr William Ury, for kindly agreeing to write the book series' foreword;
— Members of SIMI's board, past and present, for supporting the project (Mr Poon Hong Yuen, Mr Han Kok Juan, Dr Nadja Alexander, Ms Josephine Hadikusumo, Mr Michael Leathes and Ms Irena Vanenkova);
— The Singapore Ministry of Law, for being a firm advocate of mediation in Singapore;
— The Faculty of Law, National University of Singapore, for providing our students and us this opportunity;

— Phua Jun Han, for tirelessly assisting us in preparing the preliminary drafts for publishing;
— Our publishers, World Scientific Publishing, for their guidance and partnership in running the project; and
— Our students (past and present) from the Mediation Workshop, Faculty of Law, National University of Singapore, for encouraging and inspiring us.

Finally, we would like to thank you, the reader, for supporting the mission of this book. We trust you will find this a valuable addition to your collection, be it to augment your toolbox as a mediation professional or to spread the good word on furthering interest in mediation academia and research.

Joel Lee and Marcus Lim
Singapore
31 May 2016

About the CIIM Essay Competition

As part of SIMI's (Singapore International Mediation Institute) mission to promote awareness and interest in mediation, SIMI regularly organizes an essay competition to help promote mediation academia among undergraduates and students in tertiary institutions. Submissions are welcome from students not only pursuing studies in law but also other disciplines. Selected entries will be featured in an annual edition of the *Contemporary Issues in Mediation*, with attractive prizes for some of the best submissions.

About SIMI

The Singapore International Mediation Institute (SIMI) was incorporated on 15 July 2014 as a non-profit organisation supported by the Ministry of Law. SIMI is a subsidiary of the National University of Singapore (NUS) and is housed at the NUS Faculty of Law.

SIMI is headed by an international Board of Directors with representatives from both mediation practitioners as well as corporate users of mediation, to further its mission to (1) set and achieve high mediation standards through the professionalization of mediation; (2) promote understanding and inspire the use of mediation; (3) stimulate and facilitate the development and growth of mediation through research and innovation; and (4) foster a strong mediation community in Asia by engaging stakeholders in discussion, events and outreach activities.

Could Power Imbalance Be Power in Balance? Looking at Power Imbalances through a Singaporean Cultural Lens

By Ng Wan Qing

I. Introduction

The issue of power imbalance between parties to a mediation has been explored by a significant body of research.[1] Thus far, however, the conversation has been largely limited to an Anglo-centric perspective. Contrary to assumptions of Universality, commentators have found that the ideas and recommendations put forth in general literature with regard to various other aspects of mediation cannot be applied wholesale, but must be adapted to specific cultural conditions.[2] Thus, this paper seeks to expand the dialogue by considering its applicability to a local cultural context.

After briefly examining popular discourse and putting it in context in Part II, this paper will move on to consider how local beliefs and behaviours influence the current understanding of power imbalance. Part III looks at the effects of these local characteristics on the presence of imbalance between the parties. With this understanding, Part IV reconsiders the acceptability of power imbalances and offers some suggestions as to how it is to be addressed. It is hoped that this article yields a more nuanced picture of the topic in a Singaporean context.

II. Power imbalances in general

Power, in the context of conflict scenarios, has been defined as the ability to get one's needs met and to further one's goals.[3] Imbalance between the parties can be due to differences in terms of (non-exhaustive): age, gender, race, education, information, legal advice, funding, experience, personality and even moral beliefs.[4]

The concern is generally with disputes that involve individuals as pitted against other individuals or larger entities, as opposed to disputes between corporations. This essay will similarly focus on disputes of the first kind. While power imbalances similarly exist between larger entities, they can be taken to have entered into the unequal relationship of their own volition.[5]

A. Effect on suitability for mediation

The current literature generally adopts a strong stance against the presence of power imbalances in mediation. Symmetrical power relations are regarded as being optimal for effective mediation.[6] Vice versa, it is commonly accepted that strong power imbalance makes a case unsuitable.[7] Hence, contemporary literature is mainly focused on the question of whether and how power imbalances can be evened out.

Two main points have been argued, either separately or in tandem. The first focuses on the process itself and how the procedures of mediation counteract power imbalances.[8] The second advances strategies that can and should be employed by the mediator for the purpose of reducing imbalances.[9] Both assume that power imbalances undermine mediation. Even where it is admitted that power imbalance in some form is inevitable, the balancing of power in some form is still seen as desirable.[10]

B. A Western POV is evident behind these claims

Underlying the strong opposition to the existence of inequality between the parties is the notion that the principles of party autonomy and self-determination are fundamental to mediation.[11] Where one party has substantially less power than the other, his ability to participate in negotiating for his interests is compromised. The balancing of power is thus seen as a way to ensure parties are sufficiently empowered to make decisions for themselves[12] since priority is placed on the interests of the individual.[13]

This notion is a Western one, rather than one universal or intrinsic to the process of mediation in itself. According to Hofstede's cultural framework, all European and Anglo-Saxon countries qualify as "individualist" on the individualism/collectivism dimension.[14] Such cultures place emphasis on individuals rather than relationships. Further, those countries tend to measure as low power distance on Hofstede's power distance index (PDI) which measures society's attitudes towards the distribution of power. A low score indicates a societal preference for, and in fact an expectation of, equality. As such, the primacy of party autonomy and the need for power imbalance are in line with Western culture.

III. Power imbalances in a Singapore context

The different cultural characteristics of Singapore warrant a consideration as to whether the current Western literature applies and to what extent. It will be argued that power imbalances manifest in a different manner such that power disparity between parties may be more glaring than in a Western situation, but whether the situation is of concern is dependent on context.

A. *Singaporean characteristics*

Singapore is a multi-racial society, composed of 74.1% Chinese, 13.4% Malays, 9.2% Indians and the remaining being those of other races.[15] Of these, the major religions are Buddhism/Taoism, practiced by 44.2% of the population, Islam at 14.9%, Christianity at 14.6%.[16] While often regarded as a place where "East meets West", Singapore still retains its traditional Asian values.[17] It is suggested that the characteristics identified by Lee and Teh as being typical of Asian culture apply.[18] These are: (a) Confucianism, (b) collectivist inclination and (c) prevalence of face concerns.

Applying the Hofstede framework, Singapore scores high on the power distance dimension with a score of 74, indicating a highly hierarchical society.[19] This can be credited to a Confucian background both due to the predominance of the Chinese and national education efforts.[20]

The implication is that unequal relationships, or "vertical relationships" of senior and junior, are seen as the natural order of society.[21]

On the individualism/collectivist dimension, Singapore scores a low 20, indicating a collectivistic society.[22] Individuals place a higher value on group harmony above personal interest.[23] The concept of "group" must be qualified — cooperation is often limited to those of "in-groups" as opposed to "out-groups".[24] In-groups among collectivist cultures are stable and tend to be maintained even at high individual cost.[25] However, the definition of an in-group and who constitutes its members will depend on the situation.[26]

The concept of "face" comes into play here. Individuals promote harmony within their in-groups by "giving face", that is, according them the respect they are due by reference to their social position.[27] At the same time, they will act to preserve their own face ("save face"). This latter behaviour is more prevalent when with members of out-groups.[28]

The characteristics contrast with the earlier-mentioned Western notions of individual autonomy and hence warrant a re-examination of the issues surrounding power imbalance.

B. Effect on power imbalance

The effect of local culture alters the way in which Singaporean parties respond to power disparity. Generally, it serves to emphasise these inequalities. At the same time, however, some aspects of culture counteract the negative effects of these inequalities such that power imbalance is not always a concern.

(1) Accentuating power imbalances

A number of these characteristics can be seen to potentially worsen the problem of power imbalances.

The acceptance of hierarchy in society coupled with the ideology of placing society before self may lead to those with less power ceding to those with more power more easily. It is posited that in Singapore, these are likely to be along the lines of gender and seniority in terms of both age and rank.[29]

Face play may contribute to bringing about an unequal result as well. Someone in an inferior position may feel the need to give in to the wishes of the superior in order to give face to them and not aggravate the situation, especially where the other party is perceived as being in-group.[30] To do so would be proper behaviour.[31]

Face concerns may also lead a person of higher status to demand a settlement that is more than he should reasonably obtain, in order that he preserve his face in a dispute.[32] Such behaviour is plausible as the person is likely to have regarded himself to have lost face in having to come to the mediation in the first place.[33] Further, the opposing party's earlier transgression may result in him being considered an out-group, such that there is no obligation towards him anymore.[34]

Mediators who are from the same collectivist, hierarchical background may also not regard a settlement that satisfies more of the more powerful party's interests as being unfair. Being used to the social distribution of power, they would be less wont to intervene for the purpose of equalising power between the parties.[35] Furthermore, given the premium placed on harmony, they may regard the resolution of the dispute as having value that far outweighs the minor injustice of an imbalanced outcome.

(2) Counteracting negative impacts of power imbalances

At the same time however, the mutuality involved in certain characteristics may act to ameliorate the likelihood of unjustness against the weaker party even with the existence of unequal powers.

On the flip side of the duty of obedience and respect to superiors is the reciprocal Confucian value of benevolence towards and even protection of the person in the junior position.[36] If the superior does have such an approach, power imbalance between the parties does not result in exploitation but in fact helps the parties move towards a mutually beneficial resolution.

Additionally there is the trait of granting compassionate treatment towards those regarded as part of their in-group. This follows from the strong obligations towards the group in collectivist societies. As mentioned above, unlike individualist cultures where in-groups can be easily dropped and re-formed, collectivist cultures see themselves as greatly committed to their in-groups.[37]

These characteristics theoretically prevent any negative effects from impacting the power imbalance. However, it is unclear whether such magnanimous Confucian behaviours will be upheld at a conflict scenario at the mediation table with regard to a junior.[38] Further, the dispute may also have broken the superior's view that the disputant is still part of the in-group, at least for the time period. It is possible that the subordinate's behaviour in behaving in such a way that gave rise to the conflict in the first place, and allowing it to escalate to this stage, would be considered unworthy of any reciprocal positive treatment.

(3) Possible scenarios and areas of concern

We must draw a distinction between the mere existence of a power disparity between the parties and its exercise in an abusive manner. Where the power imbalance remains merely "potential",[39] the problem of unjustness does not manifest.

To sum up the above, the traits that emphasise and add to the effect of power imbalances are: the acceptance of hierarchy as a norm in society, the Confucian value of respecting superiors and, related to that, the social expectation of subordinates to give face to superiors, especially to those perceived as in-group, and of superiors to save their face by demanding more.

Cultural traits that reduce the effect of power imbalances by preventing exploitation even where power differential exists are: the reciprocal Confucian duty of benevolence as exercised by superiors towards subordinates and, related to that, the social expectation of superiors to give face to and treat preferentially members perceived as in-group.

Diagram 1 depicts the various permutations that may result between an encounter between two disputants who fit into the Singaporean cultural framework proposed above.

Cells with horizontal strips indicate situations that do not involve the exploitation of power even where one party is significantly stronger than the other. These situations are likely to be resolved harmoniously.

			HIGH STATUS			
			Strong Confucian values		Weak Confucian values	
		Seen by other party as member of:	In-group	Out-group	In-group	Out-group
LOW STATUS	Strong Confucian values	In-group	Harmonious resolution	Harmonious resolution likely	Harmonious resolution possible	Harmonious resolution possible
		Out-group	Abuse possible	Acceptable negotiation	Abuse likely (*)	Abuse likely
	Weak Confucian values	In-group	Harmonious resolution likely	Harmonious resolution possible	Harmonious resolution possible	Harmonious resolution possible
		Out-group	Acceptable negotiation	Acceptable negotiation	Abuse likely	Western-style negotiation (#)

Diagram 1.   Mediation results matrix in Singaporean context.

Cells with vertical strips indicate situations of great concern where power imbalance is likely to reach an abusive degree. In these cases, the Asian values that aggravate power imbalances are insufficiently counter-acted by those that negate its negative effects.

Cell (*) indicates the worst possible scenario. This is where the senior does not buy into the Confucian ethic of showing compassion and also views the subordinate as an out-group and disregards any magnanimity on that accord, but the subordinate views the senior as in-group and acts in deference in accordance to Confucian norms, giving face and placing perceived group interests over his own.

Where parties regard the other as a member of an out-group, or do not adhere to the Confucian values (of either respecting superiors or being benevolent to subordinates), bargaining takes place according to Western norms where individual interests take priority. The analysis of current literature applies to such cases. The archetypical scenario (#) is indicated in the last cell.

Unshaded cells indicate scenarios where exploitation of the weaker party is unlikely to occur.

IV. The question of mediator intervention

Given the altered picture of power imbalances in the Singapore context, how does it inform our consideration of whether and to what extent mediator intervention is acceptable and what forms it should take?

A. *Acceptability of power imbalances*

As mentioned earlier, the conventional view that has gone almost unquestioned is that power imbalances must be addressed. However, there are views that go against the grain, arguing that power imbalances in mediation are no cause for concern — in general but particularly in an Asian context.

One perspective is that power imbalances enable faster and better results in negotiation.[40] Rubin and Zartman observed in a study that symmetry of power produces deadlock between the parties, and produced outcomes that are less mutually satisfactory and in a less efficient manner.[41] This would suggest that imbalances in a mediation should be utilised and in fact leveraged on in order to reach the desirable outcome of settlement.

It has also been argued that in an Asian context inequalities are "expected and desired" even in the context of mediation.[42] Based on the Confucian conception of fairness and the high PDI in such countries, it is further asserted that any action to neutralise such imbalances is likely to be offensive to such parties because of the disruption of social relationships.[43] This would be the mediator, presumably from a country with a low PDI, imposing his own cultural beliefs of fairness.[44] Commentators argue that this ethnocentric attitude is an unhelpful one.[45]

Indeed, a disputant of low status and power may feel self-conscious in being prompted to assert his rights, especially where it may be rebuked by the superior or cause any loss of face to the superior himself.[46] The possibility of face-threatening confrontation where a mediator actively attempts to help them fight for equality may also be uncomfortable since direct communication would not seem an appropriate response even where there is perceived injustice.[47]

On the other hand, critics of the views above caution that mediators must not be blinded by the idea of cultural relativism, such that they allow outcomes of mediation that are not socially just.[48] This suggests that intervention in cases of power imbalance may still be appropriate. In fact, the mediator must do even more to work against such deep-set cultural norms.

It is suggested that a more considered stance is necessary rather than advocating a completely hands-off approach on the basis of the parties being of Asian culture or taking the other extreme in discounting the impact of culture altogether. It has been posited that Eastern cultures do not view power imbalance in itself as a problem, only the abuse of power.[49] It is suggested that this would be a more a sensitive view applicable to Singapore as well. Simply because inequality is expected by the weaker party does not equate to the unjustness of its effects being desired in a conflict scenario. At the same time, overwriting cultural expectations held by the parties in favour of the mediator's own judgment of fairness is unhelpful to all. The acceptability necessarily depends upon views as to the desirability of mediator neutrality as well, an issue that is beyond the scope of this paper.[50] This author suggests that intervention, even in an Asian culture, must be acceptable where the situation is an exploitative one.

B. Addressing power imbalances in a Singapore context

(1) Desirability of guidelines

The extent of intervention ultimately depends upon the objectives of mediation. Low had identified three legitimate goals: preserving relationships, promoting party autonomy and obtaining efficient settlements, while recognising that these conflict and there is no clear agreement as to how they should be prioritised.[51]

The desirability for the implementation of guidelines in this area has been espoused by some commentators.[52] If this were to be done, it is important that the unique cultural context of Singapore be taken into consideration.

Local mediation centres have already shown some sensitivity in this regard. For example, the Community Mediation Centre has a diverse pool of mediators from different backgrounds and mediators are matched to cases according to the profiles of the parties.[53] They also adopt a co-mediation model, which reduces power imbalance where one party has one or more advantages in the areas of gender, race, religion and language. Further guiding principles as to the presence of a duty to reduce power imbalance, the extent of this duty, and what actions should be taken is desirable.

(2) Suggested points for consideration

The author proposes that the following points will be helpful if intervention by the mediator is to be carried out.

First, it is suggested that mediators in Singapore be alert to potential exploitative scenarios by being cognisant of whether the parties are behaving in accordance with the Confucian values of respect and benevolence as well as whether they perceive the other party as an in-group or out-group member. This approach ensures cultural sensitivity, while acknowledging that not all parties may behave according to the "Asian rules", especially in a conflict scenario,[54] and that, at times, the rules of Asian culture may operate in a grossly unfair manner that necessitates intervention.[55]

Second, any intervention must be executed through indirect communication, making sure to help parties save face. The Singapore culture is a high-context one, which has implications on the communication style preferred.[56] An approach that protects the face and honour of the parties would engender cooperation, while being confrontational and insensitive to parties' face concerns will have the opposite effect.[57] When it comes to option generation for example, it has been proposed that the mediator should be the one to propose ideas even where the idea was generated by the person in the junior position, and to propose it in a caucus if necessary.[58]

A focus on repairing and restoring relationships may be the key to preventing exploitation. It has been seen that the treatment of the subordinate by the person in the position of power is highly dependent on whether the subordinate is perceived as being a member of an in-group or out-group. Where this perception can be altered, the problem of power imbalances can be avoided despite the existence of a power differential between the two. However, this may not always be possible to achieve.

Finally, where intervention is executed with proper sensitivity, it is more than likely to be effective as parties will be receptive to a mediator's interventions. Because of the high PDI in Asian cultures, mediators are seen to be of high authority so their recommendations will carry great legitimacy.[59] Parties would also be inclined to give face to the mediator.

V. Conclusion

The area of power imbalance in mediation is a tricky one, which many commentators have weighed in on. Exploring it from a Singaporean lens adds a unique dimension to the issue as we see how its cultural landscape affects the dynamics of the relationship between higher- and lower-powered parties.

A more nuanced examination of how power disparities may play out moves us away from both the blanket imposition of the Western-centric approach towards the issue, and, on the other end, the simplified view that power imbalances are acceptable simply because Asian cultures are hierarchical and prioritise group harmony. Instead, we see that in Singapore's cultural context, power imbalance is power in balance only in certain situations.

There is some way to go before local consensus on the issue of appropriate mediator intervention can be reached. However, with a more sensitive understanding of the topic, perhaps we can proceed to do so in a more culturally informed manner.

Endnotes

1. For key authors who have written on this, see Carolyn Manning, "Power Imbalance in Mediation", Carolyn Manning Consulting Services (undated) <http://www.carolynmanningconsultingservices.com.au/files/6514/3556/8396/Power_Imbalance_in_Mediation.pdf> (accessed 15 October 2015).

2. For examples that also consider an Asian perspective, and for the question of the role of trust in mediation, see Melanie Billings-Yun, "Trust and Mediation in Asia — The Process or the Person" (2006) *Asian JM*. See Joel Lee & Sugene Gan, "Value Creation in Mediation" (2011) *Asian JM* for methods of value creation.

3. Bernard S. Mayer, *The Dynamics of Conflict Resolution: A Practitioner's Guide* (San Francisco: Jossey-Bass, 2000) at 50.

4. Christopher W. Moore, *The Mediation Process: Practical Strategies for Resolving Conflict* (San Francisco: Jossey-Bass, 2003, 3rd Edition) (*"Moore"*).

5. Karl Mackie, David Miles, William Marsh & Tony Allen, "ADR and Injury Claims: Dealing with Power Imbalance and Emotion", in *The ADR Practice Guide: Commercial Dispute Resolution* (London: Butterworths, 2000, 2nd Edition) at 16.2.1.

6. *Moore,* see above note 4 at 389.

7. This is most apparent in cases of divorce mediation, but is by no means limited to such scenarios.

8. Jordi Agusti-Panareda, "Power Imbalances in Mediation: Questioning Some Common Assumptions" (2004) 59(2) *Dispute Resolution Journal* 24; Scott H. Hughes, "Elizabeth's Story: Exploring Power Imbalances in Divorce Mediation" (1995) 8(3) *Georgetown Journal of Legal Ethics* 553 (*"Hughes"*) at 578.

9. John M. Haynes, Gretchen L. Haynes & Larry Sun Fong, *Mediation: Positive Conflict Management* (Albany: State University of New York Press, 2004).

10. Ruth Charlton & Micheline Dwedney, *The Mediator's Handbook: Skills and Strategies for Practitioners* (Sidney: Lawbook Company, 2nd Edition, 2004) at 310.

11. The primacy accorded can be seen for example from: Standards of Conduct for Mediators, Preface to Joint Committee of Delegates from the American Arbitration Association, American Bar Association Sections of Dispute Resolution and Litigation, and the Society of Professionals in Dispute Resolution (1994). Standard I provides "Self-determination is the fundamental principle of mediation."

12. Sara Cobb, "Empowerment and Mediation: A Narrative Perspective" (1993) 9(3) *Negotiation Journal* 245. The author here however is of the view that this common viewpoint is flawed as she sees the act of balancing power is disempowering instead. Regardless, she accepts that empowerment is one of the fundamental selling points of mediation.

13. Joel Lee & Teh Hwee Hwee, "Appropriateness of the Interests-based Model for the Asian Context", in *An Asian Perspective on Mediation* (Joel Lee & Teh Hwee Hwee eds.) (Singapore: Academy Publishing, 2009) at 36.

14. Geert Hofstede, *Culture's Consequences: Comparing Values, Behaviors, Institutions and Organizations Across Nations* (Thousand Oaks, CA: Sage Publications, 2nd Edition, 2001).

15. "CENSUS of population 2010: Statistical Release 1 Demographic Characteristics, Education, Language and Religion", *Singstat* (2010) <http://www.singstat.gov.sg/docs/default-source/default-document-library/publications/publications_and_papers/cop2010/census_2010_release1/cop2010sr1.pdf> (accessed 15 October 2015) (*"Census 2010"*) at 10.

16. *Census 2010,* see above note 15 at 11.

17. Lien Le Monkhouse, Bradley R. Barnes & Thi Song Hanh Pham, "Measuring Confucian Values among East Asian Consumers: A Four Country Study" (2013) 19(3) Asia Pacific Business Review 320.

18. Joel Lee & Teh Hwee Hwee, "Asian Culture: A Definitional Challenge", in *An Asian Perspective on Mediation* (Joel Lee & Teh Hwee Hwee eds.) (Singapore: Academy Publishing, 2009) (*"Definitional Challenge"*) at 54–61.

19. Geert Hofstede, "Singapore Cultural Dimensions", The Hofstede Centre (undated) <http://geert-hofstede.com/singapore.html> (accessed 15 October 2015) (*"Singapore Cultural Dimensions"*).

20. Charlene Tan, "Our Shared Values in Singapore: A Confucian Perspective" (2012) 62(4) *Educational Theory* 449.

21. Harry C. Triandis, Robert Bontempo, Marcelo J. Villareal, Masaaki Asai & Nydia Lucca, "Individualism and Collectivism: Cross-Cultural Perspectives on Self-Ingroup Relationships" (1988) 54(2) *Journal of Personality and Social Psychology* 323 (*"Triandis"*) at 325.

22. *Singapore Cultural Dimensions,* see above note 19.

23. Law Siew Fang, "More than Collectivism — A *Guanxi*-oriented Approach to Mediation", in *An Asian Perspective on Mediation* (Joel Lee & Teh Hwee Hwee eds.) (Singapore: Academy Publishing, 2009).

24. *Triandis*, see above note 21.

25. *Triandis*, see above note 21 at 324.

26. *Triandis*, see above note 21 at 326.

27. *Triandis*, see above note 21; Stella Ting-Toomey, "International Conflict Styles: A Face-Negotiation Theory", in *Theories in Intercultural Communications* (Young Yun Kim & William B. Gudykunst eds.) (Newbury Park, CA: Sage, 1988).

28. *Triandis*, see above note 21 at 325; *Definitional Challenge,* see above note 18 at 66.

29. This would be in line with Confucianism which recognises superiority of the former over the latter in four relationships: ruler to subject, father to

son, elder brother to younger brother, husband to wife and elders and juniors among friends. These relationships are governed by propriety and reciprocity.

30. Stella Ting-Toomey & John G. Oetzel, eds., *Managing Intercultural Conflict Effectively* (Thousand Oaks, CA: Sage Publications, 2001) at 139–140; Irene K.H. Chew & Christopher Lim, "A Confucian perspective on conflict resolution" (1995) 6(1) *The International Journal of Human Resource Management* 143 (*"Chew & Lim"*) at 145.
31. *Definitional Challenge,* see above note 18 at 63.
32. Byung-June Chun, "Facework and Its Effects in Korean Firms" (2005) 9(2) *Journal of Korea Trade* 71 (*"Chun"*), at 74; John Barkai, "What's a Cross-Cultural Mediator to Do? A Low-Context Solution for a High-Context Problem" (2008) 10 *Cardozo Journal of Conflict Resolution* 43 (*"Barkai"*) at 82.
33. *Definitional Challenge,* see above note 18 at 63.
34. *Triandis*, see above note 21 at 326.
35. Ian Macduff, "Decision-making and Commitments: Impact of Power Distance in Mediation", in *An Asian Perspective on Mediation* (Joel Lee & Teh Hwee Hwee eds.) (Singapore: Academy Publishing, 2009) (*"Macduff"*) at 124.
36. Bruce E. Barnes, *Culture, Conflict and Mediation in the Asian Pacific* (Maryland: University Press of America, 2006) at 9.
37. *Triandis*, see above note 21 at 324.
38. For the approach taken towards equals — business managers to other business managers, refer to *Chew & Lim*. See above note 30.
39. *Hughes*, see above note 8 at 578 and 583.
40. Rubin, Jeffrey & William Zartman, "Asymmetrical Negotiations: Some Survey Results that may Surprise" (1995) 11(4) *Negotiation Journal* 349 (*"Rubin & Zartman"*) at 350.
41. *Rubin & Zartman*, see above note 40 at 359–360.
42. *Barkai*, see above note 32 at 63.
43. Jasper Ozbirn, "Mediating Cross-Cultural Power Imbalances—Maintaining 'Fairness' by Complying with Cultural Expectations", *ADR Times* (20 June 2011) <http://static1.1.sqspcdn.com/static/f/573702/12713888/1308090790317/06.13.11+Power+Imbalances+in+Mediation.pdf?token=Zu3tj%2Fi9HGsTXq7W5gSL%2Fpkk5T8%3D> (accessed 15 October 2015) (*"Ozbirn"*) at 4–7, 10 and 13.
44. *Ozbirn*, see above note 43 at 2.

45. Giyang An, "Enhancing the Effectiveness of Mediation in Korean-American Family Disputes: Cultural Sensitivity Training for Mediators and Co-mediation Teams", (2010) 11 *Cardozo Journal of Conflict Resolution* 557 ("*Giyang*") at 576.

46. R. S. Merkin, "Power Distance and Facework Strategies" (2006) 35 *Journal of Intercultural Communication Research* 139 ("*Merkin*") at 140–141 and 144–145.

47. *Merkin,* see above note 46 at 145–146.

48. Dale Bagshaw & Elisabeth Porte, *Mediation in the Asia-Pacific Region: Transforming Conflicts and Building Peace* (New York: Routledge, 2009) ("*Bagshaw & Porte*") at 13; *Giyang*, see above note 45 at 575.

49. *Bagshaw & Porte,* see above note 48 at 21.

50. Like party autonomy, neutrality is considered a key tenet of mediation as well. See for example Australia Law Council's *Ethical Guidelines for Mediators*. Literature differ as to how parties from Asian culture regard the concept of a neutral mediator — some argue that neutrality is still desired but in a different form, while others argue that parties are not used to the idea of a neutral mediator at all. Dale Bagshaw, a proponent calling for intervention even in Asian cultures, argues that the concept itself should be discarded. *Bagshaw & Porte,* see above note 48 at 21.

51. Joyce Low, "Promoting Ethical Practice in the Mediation Community" (2011) *Asian JM* ("*Joyce*") at 21–22.

52. Elizabeth Chua, "Procedural Safeguards to Combat Power Imbalances in Mediation" (2014) *Asian JM* at 34–36; see generally *Joyce*, for which see above note 51 at 21–22.

53. Ho Peng Kee & Gloria Lim, "Mediation to Resolve Community and Social Disputes" (2012) *Asian JM* at 7.

54. See cell (#) in the diagram.

55. See cell (*) in the diagram.

56. *Macduff,* see above note 35 at 196.

57. *Chun,* see above note 32 at 74.

58. Other strategies that can or should be adopted are in Joel Lee & Teh Hwee Hwee, "One Asian Perspective on Mediation", in *An Asian Perspective on Mediation* (Joel Lee & Teh Hwee Hwee eds.) (Singapore: Academy Publishing, 2009) ("*Lee & Teh*") at 96–97.

59. *Lee & Teh,* see above note 58 at p 76.

Mediation Advocacy: Doing Good, Doing Right and Doing Well

By Valencia Soh Ywee Xian

I. Introduction

Much has been commented about the Mediation Advocate's role in mediation, but most revolve around listing the various functions served as the client's representative. The counsel's job is not simply achieving the best settlement for one's client; it is complicated. For example, is the process undertaken by counsel legitimate and befitting of the underlying goals of mediation? Must counsel consider interests apart from one's own client? What is the "best" settlement? Does this standard gel with "fairness"? These questions warrant the consideration of counsel's duties.

Mediation is unlike litigation; even its closest cousin, negotiation, is far from the same. Thus importing negotiation ethics wholesale to mediation will not suffice. Mediation, while being a form of negotiation, connotes a much higher degree of facilitation and collaboration. On the one hand, a counsel's basic function in mediation is to negotiate for a settlement which satisfies one's client's needs and interests. But mediation is not typical negotiation. Inherently, negotiation describes "what to do" (content/substance), whilst mediation describes "how to do" (mode/form).[1] The essence of mediation is crucial as counsel's ethics and obligations are derivative. A more accurate characterisation of mediation would be "principled negotiation" — mediation is premised on the method of discovering parties' interests and generating options to create appropriate settlements. Naturally, mediation is future-focused, collaborative and value-creating.

Therefore, as mediation is a peculiar form of dispute resolution, counsel has an uncanny set of duties and professional standards. They are owed not only to their client, but to all participants of the mediation process. This paper aims to discuss the ethical obligations of a responsible counsel, explore the practical dilemmas that face such counsel and conclude by offering suggestions for reconciliation.

II. What governs counsel's conduct?

As mediation is a relatively young dispute resolution system, there is a dearth of legislation or materials demarcating the boundaries of counsel's conduct. Limited enthusiasm and exploration of mediation[2] also leaves counsel ill-prepared to deal with its accompanying tensions and dilemmas, an increasing concern with the emerging mediation advocacy practice. Unlike hard blackletter law, how counsel should conduct himself when his duties to his client, firm and the mediation process conflict is challenging. Currently, the available standards are merely suggestions and expectations of general conduct by lawyers; even so, there is underwhelming legislative or judicial reiteration. The lack and impossibility of concretised rules clearly delineating the boundaries and establishing hierarchy exacerbates the conundrum.

In Singapore, the unavailability of a specific counsel's code of conduct in mediation creates reliance on a broad, vague conception of proper conduct governed by the Legal Profession (Professional Conduct) Rules. A brief glean showcases common expectations of an advocate's conduct — to charge proper costs, complete work reasonably efficiently, act in one's client's best interests, treat professional colleagues fairly and act honestly.[3] Rule 54 best encapsulates the ethical contemplations — counsel shall act in a way that is "**most advantageous to the client** so long as it **does not conflict** with the interests of justice, public interest and **professional ethics**". Clearly, counsel owes multiple duties to numerous parties. In mediation, some of these duties even conflict. How far, then, can a counsel go to further each of his duties? Without specifically tailored guidelines, counsel's conduct is informally steered towards an ethical direction, guided by personal moral leanings. As a response to the uncertain state of affairs, this paper will explore the limits to counsel's ethical obligations in mediation.

A. *Duty to consider mediation*

Being a relatively unfamiliar domain, mediation was often shunned as a dispute resolution system. However, judicial developments have reflected an inclination towards prioritising mediation as a preferred and non-confrontational dispute resolution platform. Schemes were designed to exhort disputants to consider mediation in Singapore, including the presumption of ADR, pre-action protocols and the requisite completion of the ADR form by parties to civil disputes.[4] Counsel is arguably obliged to encourage the mediation option depending on the dispute's suitability.

However, herein lies the conflict; counsel have an obligation to advance the firm's financial interests. Besides idealised notions of affordable justice, the truth is: law is an industry and law firms are businesses. While mediation is appealing for being cost-effective, drawing one's client's attention to it contradicts the firm's profit-maximising objective. Such sentiments are universal; it was lamented that "money has a strong and insidious effect on case selection, evaluation and negotiation" and there are "potential conflicts between a client's desire for a reasonable financial resolution and an attorney's desire to operate a financially successful practice".[5] The conflict is deeply entrenched and aggravated by the practicalities of the law business, where counsel are remunerated according to their billing arrangements and requirements. One counsel even admitted the unfavourable reality that counsel's "financial self-interests often predominate over the client's interests". Undeniably, financial exigencies influence a counsel's willingness to consider the mediation option and leads him to "not realize that winning is resolving a case earlier rather than winning at trial".[6] Even with such an acknowledgement, counsel is often incentivised to prolong disputes to delay settlement and maximise financial gains. In Singapore, similar attitudes and worries against losing fees in lieu of settlement prevail.[7]

To resolve these conflicting interests, legislative efforts and measures have been implemented to compel counsel to introduce mediation as an option, effectively placing one's client before firm. In Singapore, there is a general duty to not charge improper costs.[8] This entails "not undertak(ing) work in such a manner as to unnecessarily or improperly escalate (counsel's) costs". Coupled with counsel's duty to encourage mediation where appropriate,[9] he is arguably well-positioned to grasp and perform his primary duty to his client. In Australia, a counsel must sufficiently permit one's client to give proper instructions through case evaluation and alternatives exploration, uninfluenced by any criticism or threatened unpopularity of himself or others.[10] These rules compel counsel's unwavering commitment to one's client regardless of the firm's financial considerations. In the US, there is judicial pronouncement that loyalty and fidelity to one's client is paramount and that the firm's financial interests are secondary to this first and foremost duty.[11]

However, mandating the duty is useless as counsel may downplay mediation's advantages and evaluate the option in a way that effectively discourages mediation. The solutions also assume that counsel has the willingness, capacity and capability to resist existing pressures to escalate fees. Court costs, experts' fees and overheads are systemic inevitabilities. Prevalent billing structures and high fees habituate counsel to a profit-oriented climate. The time and labour-focused lodestar approach also encourage extended billing tendencies.[12] Faced with these considerations, deliberately forsaking the client's interests seems logical. Sadly, it appears that in some cases, conforming to ethics requires more than personal conviction and honesty. Systemic reform of the firm's billing structure is necessary to target the roots of reluctance. This paper suggests firms should adopt a billing-by-efficiency, instead of billing-by-hour, approach to encourage swift and appropriate dispute resolution methods that benefit society holistically.

B. Duty to follow the client's instructions

Successfully directing one's client to utilise mediation is just the beginning of one's ethical dilemmas. Once the client has made an informed decision to mediate, the stresses on counsel mount. Counsel must follow the client's instructions, and represent him accordingly. After conveying to the client the significance of mediation and the consequences of settling, counsel cannot arm-wrestle the client into a particular course of action. Sometimes, despite counsel's advice, the client may compromise unnecessarily more, perhaps out of guilt or malleable personality. In such situations, counsel should proceed with one's client's wishes and proposed agreement. However, controversy surrounds instances where the client's instructions and motives require counsel to engage in conduct inconsistent with the profession's ethics. It is suggested that counsel may refuse to accept one's client's instructions with "valid reason" or "good cause".[13] In particular, this calls for an examination of the duty to act above board, and in good faith.

(1) Act above board

Mediation is only beneficial if there is a fair process, and that encompasses counsel's duty to act above board. In mediation, this duty prohibits making misrepresentations or omissions, especially since such conduct is convenient in positional bargaining strategies. Generally, this duty is governed by professional conduct rules and general legislative provisions regarding misleading and deceptive conduct.[14]

In Singapore, such rules are vague. Rule 53A provides that counsel "cannot take unfair advantage of **any person** in a **fraudulent** or **deceitful** or **other way which is contrary to his position as a lawyer**" (author's emphasis).[15] It is unclear if the underlying ethical principle from which 53A was derived requires counsel to conduct himself to third parties beyond what 53A requires.[16] One Singapore court implied affirmatively that counsel must serve the ends of justice and fairness in this noble profession, hence misconduct may exist even when 53A is not violated.[17] However, while the standard seems high, the duty's requirements seem arbitrary and undefined. It was even suggested that counsel may make omissions by withholding sensitive information.[18]

In Australia, the standard seems more lax. While legislation similarly prohibits misleading or deceptive conduct, counsel is neither obliged to ensure a fair outcome for all parties, nor cease to act if the client's motives are questionable.[19] Comparatively, the duty in the US is stricter and fortunately more extensively established. There is detailed legislative abhorrence and punishment of untruthful or dishonest conduct by counsel, whether active or passive. There are duties governing dishonest conduct,[20] false statements, withholding of information or even the failure to correct misinformation.[21] Interpreted generously, counsel arguably cannot over-state one's client's interests or demands to secure an upper hand in bar-gaining[22] as the client's intentions and estimates of price and value are ordinarily facts — a crucial restraint to negotiation.

Potentially, Singapore can look towards these jurisdictions for guid-ance in developing mediation ethics. This paper prefers the US' stricter approach as it better safeguards the client's interests and protects the pro-cess' integrity. Nonetheless, the inefficacy of such rules thrives. First, the definition of "statement of material fact" depends on circumstances; for example, if an untrue statement is made by counsel, but the opposing counsel is aware of its falsity, does that still make the statement a state-ment of material fact, or turn it into a misrepresentation?[23] Counsel can easily exploit such ambiguity to justify unethical conduct. Second, adher-ence to the duty is impeded when one's client has made false factual representations which has induced opposing party's reliance. Here, coun-sel is expected to clarify and disclose the truth, but the conflicting duty of confidentiality necessitates his silence.[24] In dire straits, counsel may just opt to withdraw his representation[25] should the client persist in his uneth-ical motivations and endeavours.

Altogether, if the duty to act above board boils down to counsel's personal choice, the status quo is definitely unsatisfactory. A system of checks and balances must be implemented to encourage compliance. A saving grace is the mediator's supervisory role in ensuring fair process. Upon detecting dishonesty, he should terminate the mediation.[26] But as counsel can be masters of persuasion, the keenest mediator may remain unaware. Alternatively, the self-policing approach in US is admirable; counsel is required to report another's bad behaviour.[27] Once, the Illinois Supreme Court even stripped a counsel's license for failure to report.[28] This draconian approach underlines the uncompromising importance of acting above board. Nevertheless, this approach requires a high level of proof,[29] severity and is unpopular due to its snitch-like, whistle-blowing nature.[30] Ultimately, counsel's duty of confidentiality remains threatened.

Nonetheless, this paper submits that practical considerations could strengthen counsel's willingness to uphold the duty to act above board.

Even if false statements or omissions may not amount to ethical violations, they may affect counsel's credibility with opposing counsel and can cause a court setting aside the settlement.[31] Pursuing underhanded means also risks damaging counsel's reputation in the limited legal fraternity, a detrimental long-term consequence. Therefore, a step forward is to avoid positional bargaining and advance perpetual persuasion. Counsel should adopt an inquiring mode to uncover genuine interests and pursue them honestly.[32] Also, a practical temporary solution, perhaps, is to refrain from talking numbers at the beginning — "people do not get serious about numbers until the end" as "each party just says the other's number is unreasonable".[33]

(2) Good faith

Good faith requires counsel to negotiate in true hopes of reaching settlement. This can be determined by some indicators in case law.[34] Occasionally, counsel participates in mandatory mediation half-heartedly, inhibiting mediation's potential effectiveness. Counsel may also use mediation as a distraction, diversion of resources, tactical ploy to delay timely resolution, or to fish for information.[35] The good faith requirement aims to tackle such subtle antagonism, entailing an honest attempt to resolve disputes open-mindedly and abiding by mediation guidelines.[36] Although absent of direct commitment to settlement, counsel commits to participate productively in the process.[37]

However, this duty is not free of problems. While good faith connotes a positive obligation, it is incapable of precise definition, making enforcement tricky. Also, it is not strictly imposed and the consequences of its absence seem trivial. Nevertheless, counsel should not underestimate the significance of this duty. In private mediations, the mediator's strongest coercive power in enforcement is to threaten to or actually withdraw from proceedings.[38] In Singapore, good faith requires compliance with mediation's underlying assumptions, necessitating constructive communication and collaborative, problem-solving negotiation[39]. This requires counsel to comply with obligations according to mediation's principles[40] and a lack of good faith may result in cost sanctions,[41] such as those ordered by an Australian court.[42] Hence, with good faith becoming increasingly better defined and with its broadened scope[43] and harsher repercussions, counsel should expect considerably higher standards of good faith. With a greater emphasis on mediation's principles and establishment of comprehensive indicators, counsel should meet the duty of good faith conscientiously and earnestly.

C. Duty of independent judgment

A counsel's duty of independent judgment is widely accepted but difficult to achieve due to the competing duty of loyalty and zealous advocacy. It is an occupational hazard that counsel may inevitably adopt his client's beliefs, motivations and certitude due to one's emotional involvement and desire for zealous advocacy. Counsel may be exceptionally swayed by litigious clients or clients wanting to take advantage of the adversarial system, feeling obliged to follow accordingly. However, despite counsel being well-intentioned, this misdirected professional commitment risks a lack of objectivity, reducing counsel's credibility and effectiveness.[44]

Ethical rules impose a duty to "exercise independent professional judgment and render candid advice".[45] Counsel must therefore separate himself from the client and not be intoxicated with the case's facts and ignore its doubtful aspects.[46] Despite trusting his client, counsel should maintain his autonomy, scrutinise the client's perspectives and independently verify the client's information.[47] Ultimately, counsel must resist his client's pressures and stay objective in evaluating his client's interests. Otherwise, the implications are not merely theoretical, but practical — failure to stay independent may cause counsel to give his client unrealistic expectations and, hence, undesirable advice. Even worse, real chances of early agreement may be destroyed[48] and the client may lose trust in mediation.

D. Duty as a peacemaker

Trained and accustomed to the adversarial and zealous style of advocacy characteristic of litigation, counsel may insist on entering mediation with a similar mindset. He is motivated to pursue his client's legal entitlements rigidly, in part to further his client's best interests but to also prove counsel's competency, something especially important in the competitive legal industry. As mediation seems to mean compromise, counsel often views it as an admission of weakness[49] and inappropriate to suggest when the client has a strong case.[50] Some counsel reinforce adversarial advocacy, emphasising that ethics warrant an absolute focus on counsel's duty to one's client. Discounting the need for fair process, they suggest that counsel must be adversarial, only calibrating their tones consistently with mediation's.[51]

This paper respectfully disagrees. While counsel's commitment to secure the client's best interests is important, an adversarial attitude is inappropriate as it conflicts with mediation's collaborative approach. Fundamentally different in operation, counsel's role in mediation is not to advance one's client's case solely on its legal merits, but to communicate the client's needs, facilitate negotiation and assess possible solutions.[52] Hence, mediation necessitates a calibration beyond just tone, but attitude, approach and mindset as well. Alternative techniques like creativity, patience, persistence, flexibility and resilience are encouraged without rigid or premature closure to the problem.[53] Importantly, since the "ethical reference point" is solving the problem, doing justice or even achieving Pareto optimal solutions, counsel needs to consider the opposing side as a partner in a *joint venture*, not as an adversary.[54] Adversarial advocacy's unsuitability in mediation advocacy is reiterated in Singapore[55] and similarly echoed in other jurisdictions.[56] Notably, an insistence on adversarial advocacy is a direct impediment to the mediation process. Consequently, counsel should adopt an integrative approach in appreciation of the different role, skills and preparation needed of him in mediation. Departing from maintaining strict legal rights, counsel's mindset and self-image must shift from "rights warrior" to "peacemaker",[57] and advise the client to "give and take".[58]

Nevertheless, some problems remain. In Asia, mediation and its benefits may have been improperly and inaccurately communicated, creating the perception that mediation is nothing more than direct confrontation and negotiation with a third party.[59] Consequently, a client may prefer the long-standing adversarial culture ingrained in the legal profession. No client wants a weak counsel, but some clients cannot distinguish assertiveness from aggressiveness, advocacy from belligerence and self-empowering from persuasive arguments. Hence, counsel should advise his client that needless aggressiveness is counter-productive.[60] Counsel can alert the attention of his client to Order 59 Rule 5(c)[61] to educate him on costs sanctions. And while a client's desire for strong representation is understandable, counsel can strike a purposeful balance by only engaging in adversarial advocacy strategically, to make a point or send a signal.[62] Ultimately, counsel's perception of mediation will change as mediation-related work increases.[63] Thus, the undesirability of an adversarial stance will garner consensus, influencing counsel's negotiation styles and attitudes.

III. Evaluation

A. *Importance of counsel's ethics*

The nuances and realities of counsel–client communication must be comprehended to realise counsel's practical responsibilities and power. In reality, counsel wields tremendous influence over the mediation process' success, and plays an indispensable structural role because counsel defines the problems, identifies the critical issues and formulates the alternatives. While the client remains the nominal decision-maker, counsel is the *functional* decision-maker as counsel's opinion underpins the client's exercise of his authority.[64] A Singaporean academic even noted that counsel are the most important agents of dispute transformation as they play a central role as a gatekeeper to legal institutions and as a facilitator of personal and economic transactions, and hence in dispute decisions.[65] With power comes great responsibility; counsel must respect mediation's principles, process and practice, and actively protect its integrity by steadfastly defending his ethical duties.

Nevertheless, obstacles lie ahead. First, client control problems limit counsel's influence. When a counsel–client relationship experiences an erosion of trust and confidence, a client may refuse to heed counsel's advice. Often, this results from counsel's inadequacy — overconfidence, inaccurate case evaluation and insufficient client-counselling can generate a client's distrust. In a rush to provide preliminary analyses, counsel sometimes fail to sufficiently analyse a client's case. Such premature assessments serve to anchor the client's expectations and can result in intransigence and an inability to take in new insights or information due to consistency bias.[66] Therefore, counsel must be cautious and disciplined in providing comprehensive, accurate risk-benefit analysis and disallow the pressures of work life from jeopardising the client's chance to appreciate the realities of their positions. Secondly, there may exist disbelieving or uncooperative clients who irrationally reject mediation, settlement or sound advice. Such circumstances require counsel to accept the client's final decision and respect his right to determine negotiation positions. But counsel's duties are not relinquished. He must continue to be an independent advisor and committed advocate, ensuring his client makes informed decisions by discussing the case's strengths and weaknesses.

B. Fairness

Ultimately, counsel's ethics are shaped by his notion of fairness. Hence, introducing the competing underlying principles of disputant autonomy, substantive fairness and procedural fairness in mediation is timely. While some regard fairness as disputant-determined in light of mediation's voluntary and consensual nature, mediation scholars contend that substantive fairness is necessary to achieve equity. Simultaneously, others argue that counsel has no institutional authority or expertise to judge fairness.

This paper submits that the most vital principle is procedural fairness, with which parties can make decisions that are freely and fully informed. When one's client feels he is treated with respect and dignity, mediation's actual outcome is usually satisfactory.[67] Hence, fairness and equity should be judged from the client's perspective. Consequently, counsel should seek fairness by promoting the client's interests, constantly reviewing the practical considerations of the client's decisions and the long-term sustainability of settlements.

IV. Conclusion

Despite the less formal mediation environment, counsel must always remember his professional ethics, standards and responsibilities. When these conflict, difficult decisions are necessary. Counsel must be prepared to depart from his client's expectations or desires.[68] Ultimately, pursuing procedural fairness is counsel's safest bet; yet, with time, we should not be content with this bare minimum.

Endnotes

1. David Spencer, an academic from Macquarie University, who is also a solicitor and a mediator, explains the connection that mediation is principled negotiation, premised on the idea of discovering parties' interests and option-generating based on them until suitable settlement is reached, after discovering the real interests driving the dispute. Hence mediation is based on parties negotiating in a principled way as opposed to an adversarial way. David Spencer, *Essential Dispute Resolution* (Australia: Cavendish Australia, 2nd Edition, 2005) (*"Spencer"*) at 45–46.

2. It was recognised that there is some level of antipathy or ambivalence among legal practitioners towards mediation.
   Danny McFadden & George Lim S.C., eds., *Mediation in Singapore: A Practical Guide* (Singapore: Sweet and Maxwell, 2015) (*"McFadden & Lim"*) at 72–73.

3. Legal Profession (Professional Conduct) Rules (Cap 161, R 1, 2010 Rev Ed), see Rules 13, 14, 25, 47, 53A and 54.
   In summary: Rule 13 prohibits Counsel from undertaking work in a manner that unnecessarily *or improperly escalate his costs* that are payable to him; Rule 14 compels Counsel to at all times use his best endeavours to complete any work on behalf of a client *as soon as is reasonably possible*; Rule 25 compels Counsel to advance Client's interest *unaffected by self and of firm*; Rule 47 makes it necessary for Counsel to treat his professional colleagues with courtesy and *fairness*; Rule 53A prohibits Counsel from *taking unfair advantage* of any person or acting towards anyone in a way which is *fraudulent or deceitful* [*emphasis added*].

4. Joyce Low & Dorcas Quek, "Introducing a Presumption of ADR for Civil Matters in the Subordinate Courts" *Singapore Law Gazette* (May 2012) <http://www.lawgazette.com.sg/2012-05/415.htm≥ (accessed 15 Oct 2015).

5. Randall Kiser, *How Leading Lawyers Think: Expert Insights into Judgment and Advocacy* (Heidelberg: Springer-Verlag, 2011) (*"Kiser"*) at 247.

6. Tom Baler & Sean J. Griffith, "How the Merits Matter: D&O Insurance and Securities Settlements" (2009) 157 *University of Pennsylvania Law Review* 755.

7. *McFadden & Lim*, see above note 2 at 182–183.

8. Rule 13 provides that "(a)n advocate and solicitor shall not undertake work in such a manner as to unnecessarily or improperly escalate his costs that are payable to him." Legal Profession (Professional Conduct) Rules (Cap 161, R 1, 2010 Rev Ed).

9. In reference to the ADR form.

10. Barristers' Rules (New South Wales) Rules 16, 17 and 17A.

They provide that barristers have a general duty to their client. Rule 16 states that a barrister must "seek to advance and protect the client's interests to the best of the barrister's skill and diligence, uninfluenced by the barrister's personal view of the client or the client's activities, and notwithstanding any threatened unpopularity or criticism of the barrister or any other person". Rule 17 states that a barrister must "seek to assist the client to understand the issues in the case and the client's possible rights and obligations, if the barrister is instructed to give advice on such matter, sufficiently to permit the client to give proper instructions, particularly in connection with any compromise with the case". In 2000 the Bar Council introduced Rule 17A, which states that barristers must ensure their clients have an understanding of alternatives to traditional methods of solving disputes through courts.

11. *Kiser*, see above note 5 at 268.

It quoted Federal District Court judge Harold Medina that loyalty to client must be paramount and "the head of the list (of all qualities essential to professional satisfaction and success)", despite its lack of monetary value. Attorneys also put forth the adage that Counsel's first and foremost duty and fidelity is ultimately to the client, and "not worshipping the almighty dollar".

12. Brooks Magratten, Robert D. Phillips Jr., Thomas Connolly, Renee Feldman & Isaac Mamaysky, "TRIAL PRACTICE: Calculating Attorney Fee Awards", *American Bar* (March 2010) <https://www.americanbar.org/newsletter/publications/gp_solo_magazine_home/gp_solo_magazine_index/magratten_phillips_connolly_feldman_mamaysky.html≥ (accessed 15 Oct 2015).

13. David Spencer & Michael Brogan, *Mediation Law and Practice* (New York: Cambridge University Press, 2006) ("*Spencer & Brogan*") at 203–204.

14. *Spencer & Brogan*, see above note 13 at 203–204.

15. Rule 53A provides that Counsel "cannot take unfair advantage of any person in a fraudulent or deceitful or other way which is contrary to his position as a lawyer and officer of the court".
    Legal Profession (Professional Conduct) Rules (Cap 161, R 1, 2010 Rev Ed).

16. Eleanor Wong, Lok Vi Ming S.C. & Vinodh Coomaraswamy S.C., *Modern Advocacy: Perspectives from Singapore* (Singapore: Academy Publishing, 2008).

17. *Law Society of Singapore v Ahmad Khalis bin Abdul Ghani* [2006] 4 *Singapore Law Reports* 308. It was stated that the court does not accept that the legal profession deals only with the lowest common denominator. Counsel's professionalism is owed to parties beyond those who have entered into retainer with him, and being in a noble profession, Counsel must serve the ends of justice and fairness in this noble profession. The court suggested that Rule 53A even extends the lawyer's duty over and beyond what is beyond itself also because the legal profession is not "a place where only economic pragmatism holds sway".

18. It was advanced that Counsel needs to consider when to release and when to withhold sensitive information.
    Dorcas Quek & Kenneth Choo, "Mediation Advocacy for Civil Disputes in the Subordinate Courts: Perspectives from the Bench" *Law Gazette* (2012) http://www.lawgazette.com.sg/2012-09/525.htm (accessed on 15 Oct 2015) ("*Quek & Choo*").

19. It suggests that there may also be legislative provisions that lawyers need to be mindful of such legislation as s52 of Trade Practices Act 1974 (Cth) and similar State Fair Trading legislation which prohibit misleading or deceptive conduct; this will influence negotiation behaviour. Counsel has a choice to refuse to act for a client when his instructions are for counsel to attend mediation solely for the purpose of delaying proceedings, extracting information or engage in deceptive tactics. However, there is no obligation to ensure a fair outcome for their clients or for other parties to the negotiation.
    Bobette Wolski, *Legal Skills: A Practical Guide for Students* (Pyrmont, New South Wales: Lawbook Company, 2006) at pp 452–457.

20. American Bar Association Model Rules of Professional Conduct (2002) ("*ABA Rules*") Rule 8.4.

21. *ABA Rules*, see above note 20 at Rule 4.1(a) and (b).

22. For example, Counsel may not use an overestimate of Client's needs to compel opposing party to concede more.

23. For example, Counsel may comment that Client had suffered a loss of $1 million because of the act of the opposing party. However, in reality, only $700,000 is directly attributed to the opposing party's act. Counsel may expect opposing counsel to have prior knowledge of the true state of affairs, and, thus, not clarify the details of the fact. However, this raises the issue of whether Counsel's statement of $1 million loss is "of material fact" or a misrepresentation.

24. *ABA Rules,* see above note 20 at Rule 4.1(b).
    Rule 4.1(b) states that a lawyer shall not knowingly fail to disclose a material fact to a third person when disclosure is necessary to avoid assisting a criminal or fraudulent act by a client, unless disclosure is prohibited by Rule 1.6 (duty of confidentiality).

25. *ABA Rules,* see above note 20 at Rule 1.16.

26. It states that if the mediator identifies the abuse of such process, he has no option but to confront and ask for explanation, and upon admission of bad faith or inadequate explanation of behaviour and continued refusal to cooperate, he must terminate the mediation forthwith.
    Michael Noone, *Essential Legal Skills: Mediation* (Singapore: Cavendish Publications, 1996) at 65.

27. *ABA Rules,* see above note 20 at Rule 8.3.

28. *In re James H. Himmel,* 125 Ill. 2d 531, 533 N.E.2d 790 (Ill. 1988).

29. See *Attorney U v Mississippi Bar* 678 So. 2d 963, 972 (Miss. 1996); *Skolnick v Altheimer and Gray* 760 N.E.2d 4,15 (Ill. 2000); Douglas R. Richmond, "Professional Responsibilities of Law Firm Associates" (2007)45 *Brandeis Law Journal* 199; Ellen Waldman, *Mediation Ethics: Cases and Commentaries* (San Francisco: Jossey-Bass, 2011) ("*Waldman*") at 256.

30. *ABA Rules,* see above note 20 at Rule 8.3.
    It also not only allows attorneys to report on other lawyer's bad behaviour, but affirmatively requires it. The reporting requirement is triggered if both of these hold: (1) An attorney knows that another lawyer has committed a violation of the rules of professional conduct. (2) The violation raises a substantial question as to that lawyer's honesty, trustworthiness or fitness as a lawyer in other respects. — "... crafted to encourage self-policing, it falls short of demanding clear proof of wrongdoing ... (need to have) firm opinion or firm belief ... and in terms of the gravity or severity of offence, it seems like only serious violations catalyze the whistle-blowing mandate." "... this snitch rule is also relatively unpopular", thus causing a "reluctance to file complaints".

31. American Bar Association, *Practice Skills Toolkit: Tips on ADR, Discovery, and Ethics* (Chicago: First Chair Press, 2013) at 429–431.

32. *Kiser*, see above note 5 at 235.

33. *Kiser*, see above note 5 at 211.

34. Examples of good faith are negotiating with open minds, being willing to consider possibility of agreement and not attempting to defraud opposing party. *Spencer & Brogan*, see above note 13 at 206.

35. *McFadden & Lim*, see above note 2 at 182–183.

36. Laurence Boulle & Teh Hwee Hwee, *Mediation: Principles, Process, Practice* (London: Butterworths, 2000) ("*Boulle & Teh*") at 143.

37. Counsel also urges and prepares Client to do so.

38. *Spencer & Brogan*, see above note 13 at 206.

39. *Boulle & Teh*, see above note 36 at 143.

40. Such principles include interest accommodation, value creation, relationship-oriented, future focus and collaboration. *Boulle & Teh*, see above note 36 at 35.

41. *Boulle & Teh*, see above note 36 at 346.

42. *Capolingua v Phylum Pty Ltd (as Trustee for the Gennoe Family Trust)* (1991) 5 WAR 137. The case established the principle that costs orders can be used to penalise parties who fail to participate reasonably and cooperatively in the mediation process, thus having important implications for the future behaviour of parties and counsels in mediation.

43. For instance, an Australian rule established a specific indicator of good faith. Rule 25 of the Queensland Uniform Civil Procedure Rules 1999 reiterates this when it states that: "The parties must act reasonably and genuinely in the mediation and help the mediator to start and finish the mediation within the time estimated or set in the referring order."

44. *Kiser*, see above note 5 at 236–237.

45. *ABA Rules,* see above note 20 at Rule 2.1.

46. *Kiser*, see above note 5 at 236–237.

47. *Kiser*, see above note 5 at 269.

48. American Bar Association National Institute, *Mediation Strategies: Solving Business, Tort, Employment, and Insurance Disputes* (Chicago: American Bar Association, 1992) at 2.

49. It mentioned that Counsel may also view the suggestion of compromise as an admission of weakness and therefore delay the initiation of negotiations with the hope that the onus of suggesting settlement will fall on opposing counsel. Lim Lan Yuan, *The Theory and Practice of* Mediation (Singapore: FT Law & Tax Asia Pacific, 1997) ("*Lim Lan Yuan*") at 246.

50. *McFadden & Lim*, see above note 2 at 182–183.

51. It was argued that Counsel's duty to serve Client's best interests remain above the need to assure fair process that results in a satisfactory settlement for all parties. In mediation, Counsel still has the obligation to represent his/ her Client with zeal, even if the zeal is not reflected in a withering cross-examination or a stentorian closing argument. Mediation is not a process in which the ethical lawyer lets down his/her guard or pulls any punches; it is simply that the ever-vigilant lawyer may cloak his/her advocacy in garb which is more consistent with the tone of mediation.
    Lawrence Fox, "Mediation Values and Lawyer Ethics: For the Ethical Lawyer the Latter Trumps the Former", in Phyllis Bernard & Bryant Garth, *Dispute Resolution Ethics: A Comprehensive Guide* (Washington: American Bar Association, 2002) at 39–55.

52. *Quek & Choo,* see above note 18.

53. Carrie Menkel-Meadow, "Ethics and Professionalism in Non-adversarial Lawyering" (1999) 27 *Florida State University Law Review* 152 ("*Meadow*") at 162–166.

54. *Meadow*, see above note 53 at 162–166.

55. It stated that "(t)here are essential differences between mediation advocacy and adversarial advocacy. The failure to appreciate these differences can hinder settlement or result in an agreement that is less than optimal for the client. Lawyers, who have been trained and primarily practise as litigators, must be conscious of the effects of the adversarial model and be vigilant that they do not operate subconsciously out of it during mediation." *Quek & Choo,* see above note 18.

56. The Law Society of New South Wales in 1993 developed guidelines to assist lawyers who are representing clients in a mediation and has expressly defined counsel's duty "to participate in a non-adversarial manner".

57. *McFadden & Lim*, see above note 2 at 72–73.

58. In Singapore, Counsel is advised, too, to guide Client to come to mediation with an attitude of openness and respect for the other party.
    Wee Siew Bock and Another v Chan Yuen Yee Alexia Eve & Anor Appeal [2012] 3 *Singapore Law Reports* 1053; *Quek & Choo,* see above note 18.

59. *McFadden & Lim*, see above note 2 at 183–185. It cited this observation found in Joel Lee & Teh Hwee Hwee, *An Asian Perspective on Mediation* (Singapore: Academy Publishing, 2009).

60. *Kiser*, see above note 5 at 233.

61. See Rules of Court (Cap 322, R 5, 2014 Rev Ed), O59 R5. It provides that "(t)he Court in exercising its discretion as to costs shall, to such extent, if any,

as may be appropriate in the circumstances, take into account — (c) the parties' conduct in relation to any attempt at resolving the cause or matter by mediation or any other means of dispute resolution."

62. *Kiser*, see above note 5 at 233.
63. *McFadden & Lim*, see above note 2 at 182–185.
64. *Kiser*, see above note 5 at 34–35.
65. *Lim Lan Yuan*, see above note 49 at 246.
66. *Kiser*, see above note 5 at 237–238.
67. *Waldman*, see above note 29 at 5.
68. *Spencer*, see above note 1 at 45–46.

The Facilitative–Evaluative Divide: Have We Lost Sight of What's Important?

By Javier Yeo

I. Introduction

Riskin introduced the mediation community to the Riskin Grid in 1996.[1] From that moment on, nothing has quite polarised the mediation community as ferociously as the facilitative–evaluative debate did. Proponents of the facilitative model argue that evaluative mediation is an oxymoron and therefore has no place in mediation. They believe that mediation should be governed primarily by the facilitative orientation that better perpetuates the values of mediation.[2] These are facilitative purists. On the other hand, proponents of evaluative mediation do not support a pure evaluative model of mediation *per se*, but rather, in acknowledging that the overarching orientation of mediation should be facilitative, find that evaluative conduct is inherent in the facilitative process.[3] These are the pragmatists. In this paper, I seek to debunk the facilitative–evaluative conflict. I argue that the facilitative–evaluation divide exists because of a misunderstanding of each orientation and what it encompasses as well as a lack of clarity vis-à-vis the nature of the relationship between both orientations. In conclusion, I propose that regardless of whether a conduct can be termed as evaluative or facilitative, the final enquiry must always be whether such a conduct furthers the goals and values of mediation.

II. The values of mediation

Any discourse about the facilitative–evaluative divide is meaningless without discussing it against the backdrop of the values of mediation.

A. *Self-determination of the parties*

Mediation was developed as a substitute to the adversarial process. As Waldman puts it, "Repelled by the emotional toll litigation exacts from participants, mediators seek to provide less traumatic means of resolving conflict."[4] The greatest distinction between the adversarial process and mediation is the **parties' involvement** in the process of coming up with a solution that is crafted specifically by them for them, rather than referring to objective legal rights and obligations, or other objective social standards.[5] That is the beauty of mediation being a facilitated negotiation. Parties control the outcome of the disputes.[6] Most of the time, this entails creative problem-solving based on the parties' interest as opposed to a determination of the relative strengths and weaknesses of their case. Hence, self-determination of the parties is "the most obvious value or goal of mediation because it serves to distinguish mediation from other types of dispute resolution where a third party pronounces on who wins or loses and to what extent".[7] In every discussion about what style mediators should emulate, the final enquiry should **always** be whether or not it satisfies this goal of mediation. Dorcas Quek acutely observed that "the fundamental basis of mediation — party autonomy — should not be impinged upon, *whatever style of mediation is adopted*".[8] (emphasis added)

B. *Mediator's neutrality and impartiality*

Under the umbrella of self-determination are subsidiary goals which seek to safeguard this value of mediation, such as mediator neutrality and impartiality. From the perspective of therapeutic jurisprudence, because mediation is "structured to provide enhanced disputant participation and to foster trust between the mediator and disputants", neutrality and impartiality are "ways the mediator works to gain the disputants' confidence and faith".[9] Only when a mediator is seen to be neutral and impartial by both parties will they be candid about their underlying motivations and interests. This adds to the information pool from which more creative options can be generated that address those interests.

C. Providing parties with the opportunity of exploring their interests apart from legal rights

While not an oft-cited value of mediation (at least not explicitly), I would argue that one of the key values of mediation is that it provides parties the **opportunity** to explore solutions that address their interests rather than one that seeks to clarify their legal rights. This should be uncontroversial, considering that it is heavily intertwined with the values observed above. Indeed, it has been pointed out that what is distinctive about mediation is it "encourage[s] parties to examine and articulate underlying interests".[10] An interests-based approach to mediation has its genesis in negotiation theory as propounded by Fisher, Ury and Patton in *Getting to Yes*.[11] By taking an interests-based approach, parties "may discover several possible solutions to their problem, and may also discover shared compatible interests".[12] If the most obvious value of mediation is that parties get to tailor their own resolution to the conflict, then for mediation to be a real substitute to the adversarial process that is independent on the evaluation of legal rights, it must necessarily view the interests-based problem-solving mechanism as one of the primary values of mediation.

At this juncture I find it prudent to emphasise that the value lies in the **opportunity** to explore interests, and not the exploration of interests itself which assumes a more mandatory connation. It is not necessary for mediation to adopt an interests-based approach. It is possible for a conflict to be better addressed using a rights-based approach because both parties want a quick resolution to the matter with no interest in future relations.[13] The value lies in mediation being able to **accommodate** extra-legal solutions. Unlike the adversarial process where a third party imposes a resolution on the parties based on their legal submissions, mediation allows for more flexibility for parties to reach outcomes that are not congruent with legal norms and better addresses their interests.[14]

III. The facilitative–evaluative debate

On its surface, the facilitative–evaluative debate is flanked by two distinct groups of people with a similar understanding of the values and goals of mediation, yet differing on **how** to attain these goals. The facilitative purists argue that any conduct that is termed "evaluative" is necessarily antithetical to the concept of mediation,[15] while the pragmatists push for an eclectic approach towards mediation, arguing that adopting a narrow approach towards mediation (i.e., pure facilitative) would result in a loss in value.[16]

If we strip the debate down to its roots, it is fundamentally flawed. Both camps largely agree with each other, and are really disagreeing on semantics and technical details that, in the larger scene of things, do nothing other than to distinguish themselves pedantically. The subsequent part of this paper will explore three inherent problems that fuelled this divide. First, facilitative purists, in rejecting evaluative conduct, adopt a flawed definition of "evaluative" and hence any evaluative conduct will be deemed untenable. Second, the primary distinction between both camps is that the pragmatists adopt a more liberal view towards the term "evaluative" while the facilitative purists exhibit an irrational fear of the word, and hence would go some lengths to distance mediation from any "evaluative" conduct when, in fact, both camps agree **in substance**. Third, I further argue that any discussion that the facilitative and evaluative orientations are substitutive patterns of conduct is fallacious because they are in fact complementary. The error is to confuse the means with the ends. I conclude by positing that the real test for how a mediator should conduct himself should not be dependent on categories, but rather whether or not it comports with the values of mediation.

A. *The mutation of the evaluative mediator*

One of the biggest culprits that aggravated the facilitative–evaluative debate is the flawed definition of evaluative conduct adopted by many scholars. By erroneously defining what evaluative conduct constitutes, they fail to address the real issue purposefully.

Riskin's Grid comprises of two continuums: (1) The Problem-Solving Definition Continuum and (2) The Role of the Mediator Continuum.[17] The latter is the one that features prominently in the facilitative–evaluative divide. This continuum describes the "strategies and techniques that the mediator employs to achieve her goal of helping the parties address and resolve the problems at issue".[18] Importantly, Riskin adopts the following definition for the *evaluative* mediator:

> The mediator who evaluates assumes that the participants want and need her to *provide some guidance* as to the appropriate grounds for settlement — based on law, industry practise or technology — and that she is qualified to give such guidance by virtue of her training, experience and objectivity.[19] (emphasis added)

There is no mention of **what** an evaluative mediator would focus on in the mediation, merely **how** he would do so. The purpose of Riskin in separating the two continuums was to keep distinct the approach of the mediator to the substance of the mediation, and the style of the mediator in the mediation. However, subsequent commentators that criticised the inclusion of evaluative conduct into the domain of mediation saw it fit to impute that an evaluative mediator **only adopts** a rights-based approach to problem-solving.[20] They define evaluative mediators as mediators who "are concerned with the *legal rights* of the parties *rather than* needs and interests, and evaluate based on legal concepts of fairness" (emphasis added).[21] Evaluative mediators "assess the strengths and weaknesses of *legal claims,* push the parties to *accept a settlement* and predict court outcomes and/or the impact of not settling" (emphasis added) and in doing so "perpetuate or create an adversarial climate".[22] Such a draconian understanding of evaluative conduct would obviously elicit repulsion. Indeed, facilitative purists would go on to argue that mediators should not evaluate because a rights-based approach would replicate the adversarial climate that "inhibit[s] collaboration and creativity", diminishing the chief benefit of an interests-based approach.[23] It would promote "positioning and polarisation which is antithetical to the goals of mediation".[24]

We see that a substantial source of the critics' discontentment with the evaluative orientation is derived from how narrowly they defined evaluative conduct. They created the problem to criticise it. They have confined their understanding of evaluative conduct to the "Evaluative-Narrow"[25] quadrant of the grid rather than the evaluative half of the grid. The narrow end of the problem-solving continuum where the primary goal of the mediation lies is to produce a settlement that "approximates the result that would be *produced by the likely alternative process, such as a trial*".[26] (emphasis added) Any criticism of the "Evaluative-Narrow" quadrant is understandable, for it eliminates the opportunity for parties to explore their interests, as well as overlaps substantially with alternative resolution processes such as case evaluation and arbitration. But the evaluative-narrow style is not representative of evaluative conduct. In his later article, Riskin acutely observed that these critics had "confused or conflated [the problem-solving continuum] with aspects of the facilitative–evaluative/role-of-the-mediator continuum" by assuming that "evaluative mediators would tend to impose a narrow problem-definition"[27] and thereby failed to take into account evaluative conduct in its entirety.

Thus, critics in rejecting evaluative conduct did so without a complete understanding of what evaluative conduct entails. Had they been better informed, they would have realised that the distinctions between the facilitative and evaluative were much less polarised and more nuanced than previously imagined.

B. The error of form over substance

If we peel away the layers of terminology that has vexed the facilitative–evaluative debate, we realise that the facilitative purists actually largely agree with the pragmatists in substance, yet quibble over the form.

Facilitative purists exhibit an irrational paranoia of the use of the term "evaluative" in the context of mediation. To them, "evaluative" carries with it emotional baggage that they are unsure exists or not, but dare not tempt fate by allowing its mention to even come near to the realm of mediation. The consequence is that they instead adopt **an over-inclusive definition** of facilitative, including elements which are generally uncomfortable to be there. For example, Kovach & Love in pushing for a "pure" facilitative model of mediation concedes that "evaluation inheres in every aspect of human conduct, as well as many mediator tactics".[28] They **confirmed** several evaluative activities as "essential parts of a mediator's facilitative role" such as "challenging proposals that might derail the negotiation or that seem unrealistic or suboptimal" and "*making suggestions about possibilities for resolution in order to stimulate the parties to generate options*".[29] (emphasis added) They justify that because these evaluative activities **stimulate** facilitative objectives, they "comport more with a facilitative orientation than an evaluative one".[30]

Similarly, Stulberg sought to **re-describe** the facilitative orientation by arguing that Riskin's Grid arrogated essential components that rightfully belong to the facilitative camp to the evaluative camp.[31] Drawing from Riskin's description of an evaluative mediator, Stulberg opines that a facilitative mediator should, *inter alia*, (1) be well informed of the law, industry practice or technology that shapes the context of the dispute so as to contribute meaningfully in the mediation;[32] and (2) have the ability to orchestrate the conversation to cause parties not to verbalise their actions through distributive language and lenses and to engage in collaborative behaviour.[33] He concludes by stating that the facilitative orientation as envisioned by Riskin is over-exclusive and ineffective,[34] and that the correct description of the facilitative mediator should encompass several evaluative components as observed in his article.[35]

So what are the facilitative purists really disagreeing about? The pragmatists have never rejected the facilitative process, only to "consider evaluation as a tool that can assist the parties in resolving disputes".[36] They never shy away from calling a spade a spade. They recognise evaluative conduct as it is, and prefer to delineate what would be regarded as acceptable evaluative conduct. To them, the mediation process necessarily includes both facilitative and evaluative elements, and these evaluative elements are the very ones conceded by the facilitative purists to be essential for a mediator to be facilitative.[37] A pure facilitative orientation would unreasonably restrain the mediator in his ability to mediate effectively. This is the same conclusion shared by Stulberg, who criticised the Riskin Grid for "ascrib[ing] attributes to facilitative mediators that render their service *ineffective from the outset*".[38] (emphasis added) But rather than acknowledging that mediation requires a dynamic mix of both evaluative and facilitative conduct, his obsession with terminology motivated him to subsume evaluative conduct under the umbrella of facilitative conduct he termed as "re-described facilitative orientation".[39]

Kenneth Roberts observed that facilitative purists "include so many evaluative components in defining facilitative mediation that it is unlikely they would be pleased with the results".[40] This is reflective of how the over-inclusive attitude has had a detrimental effect on the integrity of the nomenclature adopted by the facilitative purists. As we dig further, we see that both camps largely agree on **how** the mediator should conduct himself. Their polarisation on the issue is really a quibble about **what to name** it, which does not contribute much to the academic discourse other than to confuse.

C. There is actually no dichotomy

The two problems discussed above left the correctness of Riskin's Grid unchallenged. They mainly dealt with its subsequent application and interpretation. For this part of the paper, I will discuss why the existence of the dichotomy was a problem perpetuated by a flaw in the grid itself.

Riskin represented the facilitative–evaluative issue as a continuum. A continuum implies that if a mediator becomes more evaluative, he automatically becomes less facilitative and *vice versa*. It is unable to conceive of any other relationship apart from a substitutive one. However, the truth of the matter is that even "when an evaluative element is introduced … mediation *still remains* a facilitative process".[41] (emphasis added) It has been pointed out that the reason the facilitative–evaluative debate exists was because Riskin's continuum could not adapt to a scenario where it could embrace both facilitative and evaluative conduct **simultaneously**. Scholars had to choose "either/or", and not both. But we see that even commentators who took sides in the facilitative–evaluative debate strained to hint of a complementary relationship between the facilitative and evaluative conduct. They admit that in adopting a facilitative orientation, it is necessary for the mediator to engage in some evaluative conduct.[42] Thus Stempel wrote that the false dichotomy of the debate is largely caused by a cognitive error due to our obsession with categorisation. The error is that "once mediation is defined as largely facilitative, all non-facilitative mediation is classified as improper" when in fact mediation "has substantial elements of both schools of thought".[43]

Nothing could be more determinative of this enlightenment than hearing it from the horse's mouth. In 2003, Riskin admitted that his continuum misrepresented the facilitative–evaluative orientation as a dichotomy when "evaluative and facilitative often travel in tandem".[44] The dichotomy was an over-simplification of both the facilitative and evaluative aspects of mediation when it is actually so much more nuanced and dynamic than simply operating on a single plane. The fact that it is difficult, if not impossible, to properly label whether or not a mediator is evaluative or facilitative[45] speaks volumes about their complementary relationship since an effective mediator exhibits both evaluative and facilitative conduct. Examples that seek to help readers distinguish an evaluative statement, i.e., "that sounds like a pretty bus ride", from a facilitative question, i.e., "Have you considered that aspect of the proposal? Would it work for your child?"[46] are unhelpful because they do not consider the impact behind the statement or the question.[47]

To that end, however, we must be aware that we cannot conflate the means with the ends. Acceptance of the complementary facilitative–evaluative relationship does not clothe the entire spectrum of evaluative conduct with propriety. Evaluative *conduct* should be **tools** in order to aid the mediator in his facilitative *orientation*. For example, making a prediction based on the merits of each party's case and urging them to accept a particular settlement is **not** mediation. That sees too much overlap with the adversarial process. On the other hand, if the purpose of the mediator in making an evaluation is to provide a reality check for a recalcitrant disputant in order to bring him into the facilitative mindset, it falls within the ambit of mediation[48] because in the latter situation, a prediction by the mediator can "help enable the parties to negotiation in *light* of that information, and not merely in its *shadow*".[49] (original emphasis)

Therefore, if the facilitative–evaluative debate is predicated upon the existence of the continuum, logic would demand that the debate dissolves the moment we cease to see the facilitative and evaluative elements as substitutes. In other words, there is actually no dichotomy.

IV. Conclusion

In the early 2000s, Florida rewrote its professional standards for mediators by embracing a pluralistic eclectic approach towards mediation. It abandoned its previous rules of curtailing evaluative conduct in mediation and instead embraced a mix of both facilitative and evaluative conduct "as long as the mediator does not violate mediator impartiality or the self-determination of the parties".[50] I applaud this amendment. This reflects an enlightened consciousness of the State to move past the facilitative–evaluative debate and focus on what is really important — the self-determination of the parties. To harp on terminology in order to conceptualise an ideal model of mediation is to miss the point completely. We have lost sight of what is important.

It bears repeating that any discussion of style "should always be done in view of the overarching value of the parties' self-determination".[51] It is "more helpful to consider whether specific mediation techniques ... should be open or not open for mediators to use in the light of the values of mediation and the goals it seeks to achieve".[52] While delineating acceptable and non-acceptable conduct helps safeguard the purity of mediation, it is ineffective for a mediator to be unduly restrained from discharging his duty by consciously having to keep to either a particular quadrant or a particular side of a continuum, especially when (1) the continuum is itself fraught with problems and (2) mediation seeks to deal with people disputes and not legal disputes, an area that requires much more agility and flexibility. Like Florida, it is time for us to see past the petty debate and focus on what truly makes mediation a gem in the sea of adversarial processes.

Endnotes

1. Leonard L. Riskin, "Understanding Mediators' Orientation, Strategies and Techniques: A Grid for the Perplexed" (1996) 1 *Harvard Negotiation Law Review* 7 ("*Riskin's Grid*").
2. Kimberlee K. Kovach & Lela P. Love, "'Evaluative' mediation is an oxymoron" (1996) 14(3) *Alternatives to the High Cost of Litigation* 31 ("*Evaluative Mediation is an Oxymoron*").
3. Kenneth M. Roberts, "Mediating the Evaluative-Facilitative Debate : Why Both Parties Are Wrong and A Proposal for Settlement" (2007) 39 (1) *Loyola University Chicago Law Journal* 187 ("*Kenneth Roberts*") at 192.
4. Ellen A. Waldman, "The Evaluative-Facilitative Debate in Mediation: Applying the Lens of Therapeutic Jurisprudence" (1998) 82(155) *Marquette Law Review* 155 ("*Waldman*") at 160.
5. *Waldman, see above note 4* at 161.
6. Kimberlee K. Kovach & Lela P. Love, "Mapping Mediation; The Risks of Riskin's Grid" (1998) 3(71) *Harvard Negotiation Law Review* 71 ("*The Risks of Riskin's Grid*") at 89.

7. Eunice Chua, "Moving Beyond the "Facilitative" and "Evaluative" Divide" (2013) *Asian JM* 37 (*"Eunice Chua"*) at 40.

8. Dorcas Quek, "Facilitative Versus Evaluative Mediation: Is There Necessarily a Dichotomy?" (2013) *Asian JM* 66 (*"Dorcas Quek"*) at 70.

9. *Waldman*, see above note 4 at 161.

10. *Evaluative Mediation Is An Oxymoron*, see above note 2 at 31.

11. Roger Fisher, William Ury & Bruce Patton, *Getting to Yes: Negotiating Agreement without Giving In*, (New York: Penguin, Books, 3rd Edition, 2011).

12. Carole J. Brown, "Facilitative Mediation: The Classic Approach Retains Its Appeal" (2004) 4(2) *Pepperdine Dispute Resolution Law Journal* (2004) 279 (*"Carole J"*) at 281.

13. *Riskin's Grid*, see above note 1 at 43.

14. *Carole J*, see above note 12 at 280.

15. See generally *The Risks of Riskin's Grid* (see above note 6); *Evaluative Mediation is an Oxymoron*, see above note 2.

16. *Kenneth Roberts*, see above note 3 at 191.

17. *Riskin's Grid*, see above note 1 at 17.

18. *Riskin's Grid*, see above note 1 at 23.

19. *Riskin's Grid*, see above note 1 at 24.

20. I note that this is just the general sentiment. Some facilitative purists such as Kovach & Love did make a distinction between evaluative orientation and evaluative conduct, the latter being a fixation on the rights-based approach. Nevertheless, they still subsumed both orientation and conduct under the larger umbrella of "being evaluative". *The Risks of Riskin's Grid*, see above note 6 at 80.

21. Zena Zumeta, "Styles of Mediation: Facilitative, Evaluative, and Transformative Mediation", *Mediate.com* (September 2000) < http://www.mediate.com/articles/zumeta.cfm> (accessed 15 October 2015) (*"Zena Zumeta"*).

22. *Evaluative Mediation is an Oxymoron*, see above note 2 at 31.

23. *The Risks of Riskin's Grid*, see above note 6 at 103.

24. *Carole J*, see above note 12 at 283.

25. *Riskin's Grid*, see above note 1 at 26–28.

26. *Riskin's Grid*, see above note 1 at 19.

27. Leonard L. Riskin, "Replacing the mediator orientation grids, again: Proposing a 'new new grid system'"", (2005) 23(8) *Alternatives to the High Cost of Litigation* 1 (*"The New New Grid"*) at 25.

28. *The Risks of Riskin's Grid*, see above note 6 at 74.

29. *The Risks of Riskin's Grid*, see above note 6 at 79–80.

30. *The Risks of Riskin's Grid*, see above note 6 at 79–80.

31. Joseph B. Stulberg, "Facilitative versus Evaluative Mediator Orientations — Piercing the 'Grid' Lock" (1997) 24 *Florida State University Law Review* 985 ("*Stulberg*") at 990.

32. *Stulberg*, see above note 31 at 996–998.

33. *Stulberg*, see above note 31 at 1000–1001.

34. *Stulberg*, see above note 31 at 1001.

35. *Stulberg*, see above note 31 at 1005.

36. *Kenneth Roberts*, see above note 3 at 196–197.

37. *Kenneth Roberts*, see above note 3 at 199.

38. *Stulberg*, see above note 31 at 996.

39. *Stulberg*, see above note 31 at 1005.

40. *Kenneth Roberts*, see above note 3 at 207.

41. *Kenneth Roberts*, see above note 3 at 192.

42. *The Risks of Riskin's Grid*, see above note 6 at 80.

43. Jeffery W. Stempel & Kimberlee K. Kovach, "Inevitability of the Eclectic: Liberating ADR from Ideology" (2000) 2000(2) *Journal of Dispute Resolution* 247 ("*Stempel*") at 249.

44. *The New New Grid*, see above note 27 at 15.

45. *Kenneth Roberts*, see above note 3 at 208:
"In mediation, both facilitative and evaluative mediation take place together. Even critics of evaluative mediation have difficulty drawing this distinction, calling it 'the most troubling question in the evaluative-facilitative debate.'"

46. *The Risks of Riskin's Grid*, see above note 6 at 81.

47. *The New New Grid*, see above note 27 at 16.

48. *The Risks of Riskin's Grid*, see above note 6 at 79; *Stempel*, see above note 43 at 248.

49. *The New New Grid*, see above note 27 at 15.

50. *Zena Zumeta*, see above note 21.

51. *Dorcas Quek*, see above note 8 at 70.

52. *Eunice Chua*, see above note 7 at 42.

Mediating the ASEAN Way: An ASEAN Perspective on Mediation

By Jaime Lye

I. Introduction

The Association of Southeast Asian Nations (ASEAN) — a group of nations linked by geography, politics and a shared heritage — were brought together on 8 August 1967 under unlikely circumstances and certainly in the most unsettling of states. The shared experiences and cultural traits of the ASEAN nations have inevitably led to the development of a regional subculture — the "ASEAN Way", which can be a useful tool to tackle regional disputes through mediation. This paper aims to analyse the role of subculture in mediating regional disputes through 1) an historical perspective and 2) the stages of mediation. To fully understand how regional disputes are settled the ASEAN Way, the historical background of ASEAN and other cultural makeups of the region will be examined. This paper will illustrate, through the stages of mediation, how the ASEAN Way should be used as a roadmap in navigating mediations involving regional disputes.

II. Development of a regional subculture — The ASEAN Way

The ASEAN Way can be briefly described as the region's mode of regional collaboration. It focuses on three norms: 1) consensus-based and consultation-based decision-making; 2) the principle of non-intervention in each other's domestic affairs; and 3) the doctrine of sovereignty. The ASEAN Way is more than just a "normative framework"[1] conjured from thin air by the founding members. It has been developed over time and through the interaction of the member states. Apart from history, the region also shares a cultural heritage that forms the blueprint of the ASEAN Way. The normalisation of the ASEAN Way is highly significant in mediating regional disputes and guiding behaviour of the member states, hence, this part is dedicated to studying the development of these socio-cultural norms.

A. *Historical background*

At the time of formation, the ASEAN states were all embroiled in some form of conflict with one another. Indonesia was highly opposed to the formation of Malaysia (in 1963) as they saw it as a neo-colonialist plot and a roadblock in their goal of a unified Malay archipelago. This led to the infamous "Konfrontasi" between Indonesia and Malaysia. Singapore–Indonesia relations soured further after the MacDonald House bombings and after the perpetrators were convicted for murder.[2] The Philippines also opposed the formation of Malaysia due to its territorial claim to Sabah.

These events took place within the backdrop of the Cold War and the Vietnam War. However, this also unified the member states against a common enemy — Communism. Garnering strength in numbers, the five non-Communist states (Singapore, Malaysia, Indonesia, the Philippines and Thailand) felt that cooperation was needed to meet the challenges ahead of them. They recognised the need to build trust and confidence and chose a consensus-based decision-making process as the optimal way for future collaboration.

In this light, the regional aversion to external interference in the domestic affairs becomes understandable. All member states (except Thailand) had been subjected to colonial rule and hence, the suspicion of former colonial masters ran deep.[3] Thus, this shaped the development of the ASEAN Way to include an absolute application of the doctrine of sovereignty, i.e., non-interference in a country's internal affairs. These principles have been incorporated into ASEAN documents such as the Preamble to the 1967 ASEAN Declaration and the Declaration of ASEAN Concord II.[4]

B. Cultural makeups of the region

The development of the ASEAN Way goes beyond shared history; there are also cultural makeups of the region that allow the implantation of such socio-cultural norms.

Before delving into this, one must be careful not to over-generalise cultural stereotypes. This part does not attempt to use broad strokes to stereotype the unique cultural blueprints of each ASEAN member state. Further, this writer would not be so bold as to attempt to identify what an ASEAN culture is — the region is too diverse to settle on one definition. However, it will go as far as possible to identify the ASEAN Way as a subculture — a set of distinctive values, norms and practices within a larger culture.[5]

A key subcultural norm includes decision-making based on discussion, consultation (*musyawarah*) and consensus (*mufakat*)[6]. This serves to preserve working relations within the ASEAN community and to preserve "face"[7] through non-confrontational means. The origins of this can be attributed to common cultural traits amongst the different nationalities/ ethnicities of the ASEAN member states. In the traditional Chinese community, dispute resolution often involved the intervention of respected community leaders (e.g., from clan associations) who gather parties together for discussion and counselling.[8] In Malaysia, there is an emphasis on doing good, which comprises *adab* that requires the show of courtesy in word, deed and action, and *rukun* that encourages social harmony.[9] In Indonesia, customary standards and criteria (*adat*) are applied to employ consensual procedures for decision-making, especially in the realm of dispute resolution.[10] Also, in Thailand, there is a general cultural disapproval for confrontation and a heavy emphasis on Buddhist values like compassion.[11]

In summary, the doctrine of sovereignty and principles of non-intervention located within the norms of the ASEAN Way subculture stem from the shared colonial experiences of members. The previous hostilities and mistrust motivate ASEAN to establish a consensus-based decision-making process for future collaboration built on trust and confidence. The common cultural traits of the ASEAN community also contribute to this development of subcultural norms. These include a general preference for non-confrontational means of dispute resolution and social harmony.

III. Role of regional subculture in mediating ASEAN disputes

Mediation and negotiation have become avenues for dispute resolution amongst ASEAN member states. This has motivated the search for an "Asian perspective" on dispute resolution. The literature regarding this is incredibly useful in highlighting the specific incompatible cultural traits of West-oriented dispute resolution models and suggesting modified practice.[12] These are undoubtedly applicable in the context of mediating ASEAN disputes. However, given the unique history and cultural makeup of this region, should there be something more than what we should equip ourselves with?

This section will begin with a study on the use of mediation in dispute resolution within ASEAN. Subsequently, it will analyse how the subcultural norms within the ASEAN Way are an essential tool to navigate mediations in this region, using the Preah Vihear temple dispute as a prime example.

A. *Dispute settlement mechanisms*

It must be noted that mediation is seen somewhat as a last resort (before judicial recourse) in the ASEAN context. The ASEAN Charter stipulates that the first response to settling disputes include dialogue, consultation and negotiation.[13] This occurs on a bilateral level and states are often insistent on the principle of non-interference. Thus, this disallows other member states and, much less, ASEAN to intervene in disputes.

Nonetheless, mediation does feature in several dispute settlement mechanisms. Under the Treaty of Amity and Cooperation in Southeast Asia (TAC), the primary means of ASEAN dispute resolution is negotiation. If unsuccessful, the High Council will recommend "good offices, **mediation**, inquiry or conciliation".[14]

Under the Vientiane Protocol, Article 4 provides for good offices, conciliation or **mediation** that the ASEAN Secretary-General can offer with a view to assist in the dispute settlement.

The role of the mediator in disputes is stipulated in the DSM (Dispute Settlement Mechanism) Protocol: to "help facilitate communication and negotiation between the parties", with the aim of achieving an amicable dispute settlement.[15] Unfortunately, this general definition provides little guidance on what an ASEAN perspective should be.

B. An ASEAN perspective on mediation

While it is important to operate on Asian-oriented assumptions, beyond that, mediators handling ASEAN disputes must be prudent in applying an ASEAN perspective. It is also submitted that the ASEAN Way is an essential tool to form the roadmap to guide an ASEAN perspective towards mediation.

This will be demonstrated using the stages of mediation as a general structure. Within this format, this paper will analyse how an ASEAN perspective can supplement the 7-Element Framework[16] commonly used in interests-based models of dispute resolution.

(1) Pre-Mediation

(a) Identity of mediators

The mediators of ASEAN disputes depend on the country assuming ASEAN Chairmanship at the time of dispute. The ASEAN Chairman or Secretary General possesses power to be involved in dispute settlements but also shoulders the obligation to provide necessary services to address urgent issues or crisis situations in ASEAN.[17]

Thus, the identity of the ASEAN Chair is crucial as it can determine the outcome and even possibility of mediation. This became one of the reasons why ASEAN was slow to intervene in certain disputes. In the dispute over ownership of the Preah Vihear temple between Thailand and Cambodia, foreign ministers of Singapore and Cambodia in 2008 and 2010 offered ASEAN's facilities to the disputants. However, the disputant(s) refused to accept them. Also, there was no action in 2009 as Thailand held the chairmanship.

The potential delay in dispute resolution due to ASEAN chairmanship is a serious institutional problem. At this juncture, a proposal for an

ASEAN Mediation Association (ASMA) will be appropriate. An Asian Mediation Association (AMA) has already been established to create a non-political framework for regional co-operation in provision of conflict management and resolution services.[18] ASMA could feature as the ASEAN's mediation arm where disputes are referred to for mediation; a body of experienced diplomats and mediators would be involved and in the event of conflicts of interest, the particular mediator can recuse himself from the case. This system will ensure that parties who willingly call on ASEAN for dispute resolution services are readily provided with such.

(b) Pre-mediation contact

Mediators may choose to contact the parties before the mediation "with a view to establishing rapport and preparing the parties".[19] This is beneficial as the mediator can get a sense of what to expect and observe the parties beforehand.

In the ASEAN context, this rapport is built through preventive diplomacy, an adoptive means to achieve an ASEAN Way of dealing with disputes.[20] This is preferred as it accords with the subcultural norms within the ASEAN Way. Hence, pre-mediation contact translates into an on-going task of preventive diplomacy in the ASEAN context — where disputes are pre-empted and prevented through informal means.

ASEAN is one of the international organisations that host the largest number of meetings at various levels and this creates multiple opportunities for dialogue and consensus building. One ASEAN diplomat even commented that ASEAN meets approximately 700 times a year.[21] Hence, in a practical sense, preventive diplomacy works its magic through informal discussions at these formal and informal meetings. Such ongoing dialogue forms a "quiet" diplomacy that encourages and stimulates the development of mutual trust and peaceful consensus.

(2) Joint sessions

(a) Interests

In the 7-Element Framework, uncovering parties' interests is key to facilitating communication and generating options for settlement. Mediators/

negotiators are taught to uncover common interests and build towards an amicable solution to the dispute.

Mediators (in the Asian context) are cautioned to be prepared to encounter parties who may be reluctant to voice concerns during interests exploration for fear of "washing dirty linen in public".[22] In the ASEAN context, this is complicated by the fact that parties are often not operating on a shared narrative.

At the S Rajaratnam Lecture 2011,[23] Singapore's former Foreign Minister Wong Kan Seng recounted how ASEAN diplomats had worked hard to deny international recognition of the Cambodian government installed by the Vietnamese after their invasion in 1978. The Cambodian ambassador actually stood up to point out that the Vietnamese did not invade Cambodia but instead had liberated the Cambodian people from the Pol Pot regime. Hence, the clear lack of a shared narrative between the ASEAN member states makes uncovering common interests a difficult and complicated process as different countries view historical events from their own narratives.

(b) Options

The next stage involves generating options to form possible agreements. In the Western context, this is conducted in a joint session where the mediator and parties brainstorm possible options. However, *Lee and Teh* have observed that this may not be viable in the Asian context as parties may turn to the mediator to solve the problem instead.[24]

In the ASEAN context, the authority to offer solutions to disputants vests in the conciliator who can "make proposals for settlement of the dispute",[25] as opposed to the mediator whose stipulated role is to facilitate communication and negotiation. In practice, mediation often blends into conciliation, as both are merely means to achieving an amicable dispute settlement, viz., one under which neither party loses face.[26] Hence, ASEAN mediators must be prepared to play both roles and not shy away from being directive during this stage of the mediation.

(c) Alternatives

Alternatives are courses of action that parties can achieve on their own. If alternative dispute resolution mechanisms should fail, ASEAN member states can seek recourse through the UN Charter, including submission to the International Court of Justice (ICJ).[27]

If disputant(s) are insistent on seeking judicial recourse, it is vital that the ASEAN mediators test the reality of this. There is a real possibility that political opponents of either disputant will use the ongoing regional dispute to stir nationalistic sentiments to gain political advantage and support. This happened when the anti-Thaksin camp attempted to use the Preah Vihear dispute to topple the government and complicated the bilateral dispute further.[28] Such a decision must be viewed as a political one and not a legal one because bilateral ties between the disputants will always be affected somehow. Adjudication is inevitably a zero-sum game in the ASEAN context; it gives rise to a lose-lose situation where the loser loses face and the victor may lose the friendship because she caused the other to lose face. This is undesirable for ASEAN and thus, ASEAN mediators must make conscious efforts to espouse the principles of the ASEAN Way and seek compromise for the disputants.

(d) Relationship

In the ASEAN community where consensus-building and mutual trust is emphasised, the preservation of relationship after the mediation is highly valued. Relationship operates on two levels: mediator *vis-à-vis* parties and between parties themselves. A good relationship of the former empowers the mediator to bridge the gap between parties engaged in acrimonious disputes and ASEAN mediators should be aware of "face-giving"[29] tactics in order to forge good relations.

This can be seen in the then Indonesian Foreign Minister (FM) Marty Natalegawa's shuttle diplomacy tactic in the Preah Vihear dispute. Both foreign ministers of the disputants refused to meet face-to-face and FM Natalegawa shuttled between Phnom Penh and Bangkok to meet the disputants. He was also aware that the Thais preferred to keep the dispute at a bilateral level[30] and that the Cambodians would be seen as the wronged party if the matter were brought to the UN Security Council, even if they insisted on doing so.

Through shuttle diplomacy, FM Natalegawa acted as a "face-giver" and recognised each disputant's preference and need for face protection.

His efforts as the mediator were commendable; he was determined to achieve peaceful consensus and laid the foundations for such a relationship *vis-à-vis* the parties. This eventually allowed him to use his position as a mediator to persuade the Thais and Cambodians that an ongoing conflict will be detrimental to ASEAN solidarity. He also persuaded the Thais to accept the deployment of Indonesian observers on both sides of the temple border to prevent hostilities. It was revealed later that the Thais relented eventually due to peer pressure from the other nine members. I believe this can also be credited to FM Natalegawa's efforts in relationship building, so much so that the parties were willing to give "face" to him and finally close the last gap in the settlement.

(3) Private sessions

As seen from the previous section, it is possible for mediators to call for private sessions with the disputants. This occurs when the mediator senses that disputants may feel uncomfortable revealing certain information. Hence, ASEAN mediators should not be surprised when mediations between multi-party disputes consist mostly of private sessions and almost no joint sessions.

The value and effectiveness of this can clearly be seen in FM Natalegawa's shuttle diplomacy. In fact, the sequence of events reveals that FM Natalegawa conducted only sessions with the two disputants before the two foreign representatives were brought together in an informal meeting of ASEAN Foreign Ministers.[31] Shuttle diplomacy is akin to an Indonesian *wayang kulit* where the *dalang* are working silently behind the scenes to move the story along.[32] Indeed, ASEAN mediators must always keep in mind that the resolution of these regional disputes is a "matter of diplomacy more than law"[33] and, perhaps, more than mediation itself.

IV. Conclusion

The origins of the ASEAN Way can be traced back to the history and the circumstances under which ASEAN was formed. Culturally, the norms of the ASEAN Way also jibe well with the way the different ethnic and national groups respond to conflict. With such deeply embedded principles, it is logical to utilise the ASEAN Way norms to aid mediators to tackle disputes between member states. The doctrines of sovereignty and non-interference and consensus-based decision-making all have a common underlying concern: face — be it a desire not to lose face or to make other members lose face in public. The study of the stages of mediation throughout this paper also reveals that face-saving and face-giving are heavy concerns of ASEAN mediation; parties may not feel comfortable disclosing interests as "washing dirty linen in public" is considered a loss of face. The mediator generating options with ASEAN parties must also ensure that the settled options do not cause either party to lose face; this can be done through a reality testing of their alternatives in private sessions. Thus, it is submitted that a comprehensive understanding of ASEAN subcultural norms forms an ASEAN perspective that will allow mediators to perform their role optimally. It is unfortunate that the mediation in ASEAN is subjected to the strict principle of non-interference but this writer believes that with the proposed formation of the ASMA, member states can be better equipped to handle disputes both bilaterally and regionally.

Endnotes

1. Jurgen Haacke, *ASEAN's Diplomatic and Security Culture: Origins, Development and Prospects* (New York: RoutledgeCurzon, 2003) at 4.
2. *Osman and another v Public Prosecutor* [1965–1967] SLR(R) 402.
3. Walter Woon, "Dispute Settlement in ASEAN", Conference Paper (17 October 2011) ("*Woon*") at 5.
4. "Declaration of ASEAN Concord II" (7 October 2003), <http://www.asean.org/news/item/declaration-of-asean-concord-ii-bali-concord-ii > (accessed 3 November 2015).
5. Robert J. Brym and John Lie, *Sociology: Your Compass for a New World* (Belmond, CA: Nelson Education, 2007) at 90.
6. Mely Caballero-Anthony, "Mechanisms of Dispute Settlement: The ASEAN Experience" (1998) 20 (1) *Contemporary Southeast Asia* 39 at 58.
7. *Woon,* see above note 3 at 1.
   Consensus-based decision-making can also prevent the loss of "face" of other members.

8. Laurence Boulle and Teh Hwee Hwee, *Mediation — Principles, Process and Practice* (Singapore: Butterworths Asia, 2000) at 191.

9. Joel Lee & Teh Hwee Hwee, "The Quest for an 'Asian' Perspective on Mediation", in *An Asian Perspective on Mediation* (Joel Lee & Teh Hwee Hwee eds.) (Singapore: Academy Publishing, 2009) (*"Lee & Teh"*) at 5.

10. *Lee & Teh,* see above note 9 at 6.

11. Thawatchai Suvanpanich, "Thailand", in *Dispute Resolution in Asia* (Michael Pryles ed.) (The Hague: Kluwer Law International, 1997) at 261–292 (*"Suvanpanich"*).

12. *Suvanpanich,* see above note 11.

13. "ASEAN Charter" (20 November 2007) (*"ASEAN Charter"*), Article 22(1).

14. "Treaty of Amity and Cooperation in Southeast Asia" (24 February 1976), Article 15.

15. "Protocol to the ASEAN Charter on Dispute Settlement Mechanisms" (8 April 2010), Annex 2, Rule 2.

16. The 7-Element Framework was the brainchild of a group of Harvard negotiation scholars and practitioners: see Roger Fisher, William Ury & Bruce Patton, *Getting to Yes: Negotiating Agreement without Giving In* (New York: Penguin, 2nd Edition, 1991).

17. *ASEAN Charter*, Article 32(c).

18. Teh Hwee Hwee, "Mediation Practices in ASEAN: The Singapore Experience" (Paper delivered at the 11th General Assembly of the ASEAN Law Association on 17 February 2012) at 25, <http://www.aseanlawassociation.org/11GAdocs/workshop5-sg.pdf> (accessed 3 November 2015).

19. *Lee and Teh,* see above note 9 at 75.

20. ASEAN Regional Forum, "ASEAN Regional Forum Concept and Principles of Preventive Diplomacy" < http://aseanregionalforum.asean.org/library/arf-chairmans-statements-and-reports.html?id=159 > (accessed 3 November 2015).

21. Roxana Cristescu, Augustin Nicolescou & Agus Wandi, "ASEAN and Peace Mediation: Progress, Challenges, and Co-operation" (Paper based on the conference "ASEAN–EU High-Level Expert Workshop on Preventive Diplomacy and International Peace Mediation" held in Bali, Indonesia on 11 October 2011) (*"ASEAN and Peace Mediation"*) at 9.

22. *Lee & Teh,* see above note 9 at 83.

23. Held at the Shangri-La Hotel, Singapore on 23 November 2011 (*"S Rajaratnam Lecture"*).

24. *S Rajaratnam Lecture,* see above note 23.

25. "Protocol to the ASEAN Charter on Dispute Settlement Mechanisms" (8 April 2010), Annex 3, Rule 3(3).
26. *Woon,* see above note 3 at 19.
27. This is explicitly recognised in Article 28 of the ASEAN Charter and Article 17 of the TAC in Southeast Asia. Submission to the ICJ has been used several times, such as in the Sipadan/Litigan dispute and the Pedra Branca dispute.
28. International Crisis Group Asia Report No. 215, *Waging Peace: ASEAN and the Thai-Cambodia Border Conflict* (6 December 2011) at 9.
29. Eric van Ginkel, "The Mediator as Face-Giver" (2004) 20 *Negotiation Journal* 475.

    The mediator as a "face-giver" may compliment, acknowledge the merits, achievements and contributions of parties and give other forms of recognition.
30. *Woon,* see above note 3 at 25.
31. This was held on 22 February 2011 in Jakarta.
32. *Wayang kulit* refers to the ancient form of storytelling from Java and uses handcrafted puppets projected in front of a screen lit from behind. *Dalang* refers to the master puppeteer who manipulates the puppets using the attached sticks. UNESCO, "Wayang Puppet Theatre" <http://www.unesco. org/culture/ich/RL/00063?> (accessed 3 November 2015).
33. *Woon,* see above note 3 at 30.

Faces of Singapore & Mediation

By Joey Lim Yue Tow

I. Introduction

Much has been written on the importance of face in relation to communicative behaviour and by extension, to mediation. Even more perhaps, has been written on the fundamental difference between the Western and Asian concepts of "face", *mien-tzu*[1] (面子 — Mian [4] Zi [3]) and *lien* (脸 — Lian [3]).[2] Singaporeans have traditionally been treated in academic research to have an "Asian" concept of face.[3]

This paper hopes to show that a Singaporean concept of face cannot simply be type-cast as either "Western" or "Asian". In identifying a unique Singaporean concept of "face", the paper also hopes to explore the different styles of dispute resolution of the two neglected minority races in Singapore, the Malays and Indians.

Lastly, this paper will offer some practical implications of using the uniquely "Singaporean" face within mediation itself.

II. A Singaporean concept of face: neither Western nor Asian

It seems necessary to first debunk the assumption that Singapore's concept of face should be type-cast as "Asian". It would be instructive to turn to the determinants of "face". "Face" has been inextricably linked to culture,[4] societal predisposition towards collectivism or individualism, power-distance,[5] amongst other factors.

It should be noted that, in the particular context of mediation, Singapore has been considered alongside countries such as China, Japan, Korea and Vietnam and Ng has concluded that Singapore was "unlikely to be an exception."[6] It seems that the basis of this statement is largely attributable to Singapore's largely Chinese ethnographic structure.

This paper argues that the multi-ethnic nature of Singapore should negate this conclusion. For example, it has been noted that the different ethnic groups in Singapore have different "approaches" in dealing with problems, which is arguably representative of a different concept of face as between different ethnic groups.[7] Further, Ting-Toomey, the modern founder of face negotiation theory, does support having a modified "image of self and concerns with face", particularly in an ethnically diverse culture.[8] Put another way, it is incorrect to assume that the Singaporean concept of face is similar to the stereotypical "Asian" concept.

The exact nature of multi-ethnicity on Singapore's concept of face will be explored in the next section. However, as an illustrative example of how Singaporean culture is vastly different from the Chinese, Chinese society is uniquely characterised as placing an undue emphasis on *guanxi* (关系 — Guan [1] Xi [4]), which translates into a "relationship building system",[9] this *guanxi* is often characterised as ubiquitous in China and often has implications on corruption at both the micro and macro level.[10] Singaporeans, however, have a different concept of *guanxi,* even going so far as to reject it.[11] Singapore is characterised as a society unforgiving and free of corruption, complying with international standards such as those of Transparency International and Political and Economic Risk Consultancy.

Further, Singapore has been popularly described as a "midway" between China and the United States, in terms of cultural orientation towards dispute resolution.[12] This is, in my view, due to our predominantly Chinese population, but distinctly Western education system. It has even been argued that the cultural orientation of Singaporeans can and should be independently ascertainable.[13] References to Western/Asian divergence or Chinese/Asian cultures are and should only be made for the sake of convenience in understanding. We next turn to features that contribute to a unique Singaporean "face".

III. Singaporean concept of face

Face has been defined as a "something that is diffusedly located in the flow of events".[14] Whilst this might be an overly generic definition, it does lend credence to the idea that face is determined by the circumstance; "face is a mask that changes depending in the audience and the variety of social interaction."[15] In the particular context of mediation, face is perhaps better defined as "a psychological image that can be granted, lost, fought for and presented as a gift".[16]

Drawing from the previous determinants of face, I will examine Singapore's culture, societal disposition towards collectivism or individualism, and power distance in turn to examine their effects on Singapore's concept of face.

Culture, in the Singapore context, is a shared way of life — the behaviours, beliefs, values, languages and symbols that we accept, generally without conscious thought and that are passed on by communication and imitation from one generation to the next.[17]

Defining a Singapore culture can be problematic because there are four distinct ethnic groups in Singapore, all of which exhibit cultural differences. It is therefore useful to determine shared values or behaviours that transcend ethnic differences and are common to Singaporeans, irrespective of ethnicity.

"Kiasu-ism" has been defined as a "national fixation in Singapore".[18] Despite its fundamentally Chinese roots, it has diffused across all ethnicities in Singapore, perhaps due to the emphasis on meritocracy within Singapore. To be "kiasu" (literally "afraid to lose" in the Hokkien dialect) is to have the "obsessive need to get the most out of every transaction and the desire to get ahead of others".[19]

This is well observed through the "chope"ing (reserving, in local parlance) of seats in hawker centres with the use of tissues, or the inane rush to obtain a seat on the train during peak hour.

Yet what makes "kiasu-ism" a distinctly individualistic trait, truly significant in the context of Singapore, is how it squares with the supposedly "collectivist" nature of Singapore.[20] With a Geert Hofstede Individualism score of 20, Singapore ranks highly as one of the most collectivist countries in the world.

This paper submits that "kiasu-ism" is congruent with collectivism in the sense that "kiasu" behaviour is often engaged in because each individual sees himself as part of a larger "group" and seeks the maximum "rate of returns" from their behaviour as a member of that group.

To illustrate this point, the use of tissues to reserve seats in hawker centres is to allow every member of their "lunch group" to purchase food at the same time, eliminating the need for one member of the group to be left behind to reserve the table.[21] Train commuters often rush in to reserve seats for their friends or family, and even children engage in tuition primarily to satisfy their parents.

Therefore what makes "kiasu-ism", *vis-à-vis* the Chinese concepts of *lien* or *mian-tzu,* truly unique to a Singaporean concept of face is the fact that an individual's "face" can often be sacrificed for the material welfare of a group and, more significantly, the fact that this is socially accepted or even desirable.[22]

This deviates from the Chinese conception of *lien* as the "consciousness of moral boundaries, which maintain moral values and expresses the force of social sanctions".[23] Significantly, a Singaporean might be willing to forego *lien* in order to achieve an advantage for the group he identifies with.

"Ethnic Compartmentalisation & Respect" can arguably form a crucial aspect of "face" perception, especially in conflicts or mediations as between parties of different ethnicities. Singapore's multicultural make-up and historical sensitivity to different cultures or races force Singaporeans to treat people of different ethnic groups differently.[24]

An illustrative example is the furore of criticism and argument that arose when it was reported in the news in 2011 that a mediated community dispute resulted in an Indian family agreeing to cook curry only on days that their Chinese neighbour was not at home. It later turned out that the resolution was voluntarily agreed into for the sake of racial harmony and was not recommended by the mediator, as was alleged by critics of the outcome.

Notwithstanding the misunderstanding of the role of the Community Mediation Centre and the mediators in the above dispute, this case illustrates that where cross-ethnic disputes occur, especially over practices that are considered ethnical or cultural, Singaporean parties tend to emphasize "face-giving" in conflict resolution.[25]

More than a particular style in conflict resolution, it can be attributed to Singaporeans compartmentalizing each other into four "main races" in a way similar to how the State organises the citizenry along the CMIO model (Chinese–Malay–Indian–Others).[26] In the process of compartmentalisation, we associate certain actions or cultural practices/identifiers with the group that are "inviolable". In doing so, we construct a uniquely Singaporean "face", especially in relation to conflicts over culture or cultural practices, i.e., we see ourselves as Singaporeans giving respect to other Singaporeans because of ethnic differences.

IV. Malay and Indian styles of dispute resolution

Singapore has traditionally been viewed as a "Confucian" country, particularly in conflict resolution, despite its ethnic diversity. This paper argues that the concept of a "Singaporean" face cannot be complete without inclusion of all its constituent ethnic groups.[27] The following discussion will therefore focus on the differences as between the "Chinese" culture and the Malay and Indian culture in dispute resolution.

Perhaps one of the reasons this has been neglected is because of the similarities of Malay and Indian culture in being contributing factors to the overview of Singaporeans being collectivist in nature, with a high power distance ratio and valuing "face".[28] Even then, this paper argues that a deeper understanding of Malay and Indian "face" should be understood so as to facilitate a more harmonious cross-cultural mediation scene within Singapore.

Singaporean Malays are highly influenced by Islam and it has even been argued that it forms part of their national identity.[29] This translates into an emphasis on patience and a similar emphasis on *budi* and *adat*, the latter being a shared set of **internal** values that formulates norms of social behaviour of Malay individuals. *Budi* emphasises "intuitive feelings",[30] and mutual tolerance.

Singaporean Indians on the other hand are characterised as "idealistic" due to the influence of Brahmanism;[31] this "idealism" translates into a focus on the long term and relationship building and sustenance. A focus on the philosophical underpinnings of actions might translate into a higher level of moral judgment on actions. Moreover, it has been stated that the Indian style of negotiation, whilst acknowledging the importance of face and relationship building, places less emphasis on it as compared to Chinese/Singaporean society.[32]

This has translated into tangibly different styles: Singaporean Malays have been described to be more empathetic and emotional in negotiations, but might not adhere completely to a rigid structure of negotiation.[33] Singaporean Indians can come across as more individualistic and more achievement-oriented as compared to the rest of the ethnicities, if not operating in what they perceive as an "in-group".[34]

Having summarised some salient differences as between the ethnic groups, Table 1 sets out this author's opinions as to how to better deal with these differences in mediation.

Table 1. How to better deal with ethnic differences in mediation

Chinese	1. Place the greatest emphasis on face of all three ethnic groups; care must be taken not to undermine authority or respect
	2. Might be instrumental to remove perceived persons of authority in order to elicit full disclosure from junior employees
	3. Be aware that Chinese employees, especially high-ranking employees, tend to identify with their company's interests as their own
	4. Avoid criticism or negative framing of their company's actions
Indian	1. Strongly principled and might not be willing to budge on certain "moral" aspects of actions; tend to focus on normative value of actions rather than consequences
	2. Might be useful to establish value in a "long-term" scenario, to establish "insider" status
	3. "Long-term" view is conducive to creating sustainable and practical solutions
	4. Might be more confrontational than other ethnic groups, so more control would be needed from the mediator
Malay	1. Do not focus too much on rigid structure of mediation as deviation from rigid plans might be conducive to exploring interests
	2. Focus on reciprocity element of mediation
	3. Address emotionality as representation of interest

It is not submitted that the above conclusions are entirely to be relied on, due to the fact that mediation parties vary in terms of being culturally influenced and the danger of generalisation. However, the author does hope that the above table provides a rough framework for recognition of cultural differences as between Singaporeans.

V. A distinct Singaporean mediation style

It is significant to acknowledge similarities as well, insofar as there are tangible differences between the various ethnic groups within Singapore, we arguably retain distinctive elements of being Singaporean within our styles of dispute resolution. More specifically, this section examines how the common element of "kiasu-ism" translates into mediation.

There are two academically recognised manifestations of "kiasu-ism", kiasu-positive and kiasu-negative.[35] Kiasu-positive behaviours are actions undertaken to establish value, through diligence and hard work. Kiasu-negative behaviours are actions that emphasise selfishness and guile.[36]

For example, kiasu-positive behaviour could be undertaken in mediation when one party offers viable options in resolving the dispute, creating value for both parties, or when they reaffirm and recognise the value that the counter-party has created for them in prior transactions. Kiasu-negative behaviour, on the other hand, could manifest itself in one party exaggerating the harm done to his company, in order to achieve a larger compensation or exaggerating the hurt he feels in order to gain sympathy.

It is perhaps unsurprising that kiasu-negative behaviour has been examined to be maladaptive and dysfunctional in group-based tasks.[37] Kiasu-positive behaviour manifests itself when Singaporeans see the party as an "insider" or part of their group whereas kiasu-negative behaviour manifests itself significantly when Singaporeans see the other party as the "person to get ahead of".[38]

Beyond kiasu-ism, Singaporeans are typified as having high respect for authority,[39] with a preference for indirectness in both communication and resolution of conflict, and with a profound respect for ethnical differences.

VI. Recommendations

This paper acknowledges that mediators need to be flexible, to suit the diverse nature of disputants that he comes across. This paper however seeks to use the characteristics of Singaporean "face" and its cultural orientation towards dispute resolution to recommend changes where suitable, in a matter which the mediators can control, the seating arrangement within mediation.[40]

Using seating arrangements to gain symbolic power or to influence parties is not uncommon; for example, a judge in a courtroom is almost always elevated in relation to the parties. Space is created as between victim witnesses and an accused perpetrator.

It is worth noting that the typical "Western" seating arrangement for mediation is as follows in Figure 1.

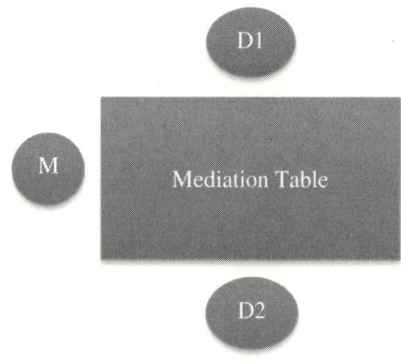

Figure 1.   Western seating arrangement for mediation.

A. *Benefits/Shortcomings of the Figure 1 arrangement*

This allows mediators to address Disputants [D1 & D2] from a neutral perspective.

This confers authority on the Mediator (M) as in the Asian context; the head of the "household" usually sits at the head of the table.

This accords well with Singaporeans' respect of hierarchy of power and might give mediators more authority to work with.

This allows disputants to "see each other to watch facial and body expressions".[41] This might allow disputants to show emotionality and might do well in scenarios where one party feels like they need to directly apologise or directly address their counter-party.

On the other hand, having disputants facing each other might well make the mediation more adversarial. Singaporeans are more in favour of indirectness in dispute resolution.[42]

This might encourage kiasu-negative behaviour as it raises the tendency for disputants to see each other as adversaries instead of collaborators.[43] As discussed, this increases the tendency to "compete" against perceived adversaries by engaging in guile and deceit if deemed necessary.

Allowing disputants to see each other's body language might be more detrimental than useful in cross-cultural mediation settlements. Non-verbal cues are susceptible to misinterpretation; for example, using your

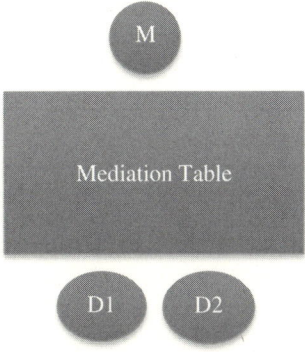

Figure 2.   Recommended seating arrangement for mediation in Singapore.

left hand (especially your forefinger) to point at something is considered discourteous in Malay culture.[44] One can only imagine the misunderstandings that might occur if a counter-party were to be left-handed. While it has been discussed that Singaporeans have deep respect for ethnic differences, it is perhaps limited to cultural practices that Singaporeans have knowledge of. Further, with the propensity for international mediation rising and hence the engagement of international parties, it might be prudent to assume that not all parties know of significant non-verbal cues.

This paper recommends that the seating arrangement depicted in Figure 2 would be more suitable for mediation within Singapore, involving at least one Singaporean party.

B. Benefits/Shortcomings of the Figure 2 arrangement

The mediator is still ostensibly neutral as he should be seated on the other side of the table, but "in between" and equidistant from the two disputants. This arguably maintains the leadership role of the Mediator because he is able to maintain eye contact with both disputants and is "visually central".[45]

This allows the Mediator to better observe all features of non-verbal cues that disputants might be giving off and allows him to better gauge their feelings and emotions at any point of time. Simultaneously, the onus on "being non-verbally culturally sensitive" shifts to the mediator who is in a better position to know cultural taboos of disputants than the disputants themselves.

Most significantly, this better creates an atmosphere of collaboration and reduces the tendency of disputants to see the other disputant as "other" or as an adversary.[46] This thereby reduces the predisposition for "kiasu-negative" behaviour to manifest,[47] and increases the potential for "kiasu-positive" behaviour because disputants are not physically "pitted against each other". On the other hand, this arrangement might not be suitable for parties that are emotionally uncomfortable with physical proximity, e.g., family mediation sessions. Disputants might feel initially uncomfortable with being seated right next to each other, but this can be easily managed through the mediator's directions.

If it should be necessary to introduce a co-mediator, co-mediators should sit beside each other to symbolise an equal partnership that disputants would tend to emulate.[48]

Lawyers/legal advocates should sit beside the disputants on the side of the table facing the mediators. However, it is crucial to ensure that parties remain in the "centre" of the table, as they would be the symbolic "centre" driving force of the process.

VII. Conclusion

Singaporeans are neither truly "Western" nor truly "Asian" in our approach towards conflict resolution or in our construct of "face". It follows that our concept of mediation itself should be unique. There has been a dearth of research into the precise repercussions of our unique heritage on mediation and we have traditionally been type-cast because of our Chinese ethnography. This paper hopes to have dispelled the requirement for such "type-casting" and to have laid down the foundations for a "Singaporean" identity within mediation.

Endnotes

1. Hsien Chin Hu, "Chinese Concepts of 'Face'", *American Anthropologist* (1994) 46(1), 45–64 ("*Hsien*").
2. The words and numbers in parentheses denote how to pronounce the Chinese characters according to the 汉语拼音 (Han [4] Yu [3] Pin [1] Yin [1]) system

of phonetic transcription. For more information, see http://en.wikipedia.org/wiki/Pinyin (accessed 15 October 2015).

3. Joel Lee & Teh Hwee Hwee, *An Asian Perspective on Mediation* (Joel Lee & Teh Hwee Hwee eds.) (Singapore: Academy Publishing, 2009) at Chapter 7.

4. Stella Ting-Toomey, "Intercultural Conflict Styles: A Face Negotiation Theory", in *Theories in Intercultural Communication* (Young Yun Kim and William B. Gudykunst eds.) (Newbury Park, CA: Sage, 1988) (*"Ting-Toomey 1988"*) at 213–235.

5. Power distance is the extent to which the less powerful members of organisations and institutions (like the family) accept and expect that power is distributed unequally. Geert Hofstede, *Culture's Consequences: International Differences in Work-Related Values* (Newbury Park, CA: Sage Publications, 1980).

6. John Ng, "Four Faces of Face: Implications for Mediation", a paper presented at the 2nd Mediation Conference at the National University of Singapore (1998).

7. Adrian Loke, "Mediation in the Singapore Family Court" (1999) 11 *Singapore Academy of Law Journal* 189 at 204.

8. Stella Ting-Toomey, "The Matrix of Face: An Updated Face Negotiation Theory", in *Theorizing about Intercultural Communication* (William B. Gudykunst ed.) (Thousand Oaks, CA: Sage Publications, 2005) at 71–92.

9. Ming-Cheng M. Lo & Eileen M. Otis, "Guanxi Civility: Processes, Potentials, and Contingencies" (2003) 31(1) *Politics & Society* 131.

10. Ling Li, "Performing Bribery in China: guanxi-practice, corruption with a human face" (2011) 20(68) *Journal of Contemporary China* 1.

11. Haoxiang Cai, "No Guanxi Please: We're Singaporeans", *The Straits Times* (8 October 2009).

12. Lim Lan Yuan, "Impact of Cultural Differences on Dispute Resolution" (1996) 7 *Australasian Dispute Resolution Journal* 197.

13. Lim Lan Yuan, "Mediation Styles and Approaches in Asian Culture", in *Conference Proceedings of the 2nd Asia Pacific Mediation Forum: Developing a Mediation Culture*, Singapore (19–22 November 2003).

14. Erving Goffman, "On Face-Work: An Analysis of Ritual Elements in Social Interaction" (1955) *Psychiatry: Journal for the Study of International Processes* 213.

15. Erving Goffman, *Interaction Ritual: Essays on Face-to-face Behavior* (New York: Anchor Books, 1967).

16. Lin Yutang, *My Country and My People* (New York: John Day, 1968).

17. Robert J. Brym & John Lie, *Sociology: Your Compass for a New World* (Belmont: Thomson Wadsworth Publishing, 3rd Edition, 2007).
18. *MacQuarie Dictionary* (Sydney: Macquarie Library Pte Ltd, 3rd Edition, 1997).
19. Alvin Hwang, Soon Ang & Anne Marie Francesco, "The Silent Chinese: The Influence of Face and Kiasuism on Student Feedback-Seeking Behaviors" (2002) 26 *Journal of Management Education* 70 (*"Hwang"*).
20. Jackie Jie Qi Ooi, "A Singapore way of life: an investigation into kiasu-ism as a way of Life" (2013) NTU HSS Student Reports (final year project).
21. Linda Yan Zhangting, "Tissue system's a time saver", *Today* (17 April 2007).
22. See for example, Eric G. Kirby & John K. Ross, "Kiasu Tendency and Tactics: A Study of Their Impact on Task Performance" (2007) 8(2) *Journal of Behavioral and Applied Management* 108 (*"Kirby and Ross"*).
23. *Hsien,* see above at note 1.
24. Chan Sek Keong, "Multiculturalism in Singapore: The way to a harmonious society" (2013) 25 *Singapore Academy of Law Journal* 84.
25. K. Shanmugam said, "It's heartening to see so many people come together to affirm a key aspect of the way Indians lead their lives in Singapore."
    Karen W. Lim, "Families settle curry dispute, not mediators", *Asiaone* (16 August 2011) <http://news.asiaone.com/News/AsiaOne+News/Singapore/Story/A1Story20110816-294757.html> (accessed 15 October 2015).
26. Nur Diyanah Anwar, "Immigration and the Singaporean identity: The Ethnicity Conundrum", RSIS Commentary No. 211 (27 October 2011).
27. It is with deep regret that I exclude the "Others" racial group in this analysis because although the 4th group has traditionally been Eurasian, the influx of immigrants being lumped under "Others" has diversified into such a large variety that it becomes hard to unify them under a common culture.
28. The similarities have been explored comprehensively.
    Nik Maheran Nik Muhammad & Filzah Md Isa, "Impact of Culture and Knowledge Acquisition to Organizational Success" (2009) 1(2) *Asian Culture and History* 63.
29. Syed M. Khairudin Aljunied, "Making Sense of an Evolving Identity: A Survey of Studies on Identity and Identity Formation among Malay-Muslims in Singapore", (2006) 26(3) *Journal of Muslim Minority Affairs* 371.
30 Wan Norhasniah Wan Husin, "Budi-Islam; It's role in the construction of Malay identity in Malaysia" (2011) 1(12) *International Journal of Humanities and Social Sciences* 132.
31. Rajesh Kumar, "Brahmanical Idealism, Anarchical Individualism, and the Dynamics of Indian Negotiating Behaviour" (2004) 4 *International Journal of Cross Cultural Management* 39.

32. Michael Benoliel, "Negotiating Successfully in Asia" (2013) 1(1) *Eurasian Journal of Social Sciences* 1 ("*Benoliel*").

33. AAhad M. Osman-Gani & Joo-Seng Tan, "Influence of culture on negotiation styles of Asian managers: An empirical study of major cultural/ethnic groups in Singapore" (2002) 44 *Thunderbird International Business Review* 819 ("*Osman-Gani*").

34. *Benoliel*, see above at note 34.

35. Alvin Hwang, "Adventure Learning: Competitiveness (Kiasu) Attitudes and Teamwork", (2003) 22 (7/8) *Journal of Management Development* 562.

36. *Hwang*, see above at note 21.

37. *Kirby and Ross,* see above at note 24.

38. *Hwang*, see above at note 21.

39. Geert Hofstede statistics, Power Distance Index of 74.

40. For reasons of required brevity, only a traditional rectangle table will be considered.

41. Rebecca Jane Weinstein, *Mediation in the Workplace: A Guide for Training, Practice and Administration* (Westport, CT: Quorum Books, 2001) at 81.

42. *Osman-Gani*, see above at note 35.

43. L. Schirch, *Ritual and Symbol in Peacekeeping* (Kumarian Press, 2004) at 68 ("*Schirch*").

44. T. Morrison & W.A. Conaway, *Kiss, Bow or Shake Hands: Best Selling Guide to Doing Business in More Than 60 Countries* (Avon, MA: Adams Media Publications, 2nd Edition, 2006).

45. Carol Kinsey Goman, "Want Collaboration? Watch Where You Sit", *Forbes* (2 April 2012) <http://www.forbes.com/sites/carolkinseygoman/2012/04/02/want-collaboration-watch-where-you-sit/> (accessed 15 October 2015) ("*Goman*").

46. *Schirch,* see above at note 45; *Goman*, see above at note 47.

47. *Hwang*, see above at note 21.

48. Michael T. Colatetrella, Jr & Anthony P. Picchioni, *Mediation: Skills and Techniques* (LexisNexis Publishing, 2008).

Manipulation in Mediation

By Koh Zhen Yang

I. Introduction

This essay examines the various dimensions of manipulation in mediation, focusing specifically on the definition of manipulation and its exercise in mediation, the mediator paradox and, finally, how manipulation can be managed in mediation.

II. Definition(s) of manipulation

The dictionary definition of manipulation is a helpful starting point to understand its meaning in the context of mediation. Interestingly, two distinct definitions for manipulation are offered:[1]

1. The action of manipulating something in a skilful manner
2. The action of manipulating someone in a clever or unscrupulous way

Both definitions make an implied reference to the ability of a person to modify or alter the end result of a situation — whether it is by manipulating the process or the party to reach an outcome.

It has been said that the very presence of the mediator transforms the dispute into a three-way dialogue whereby the mediator is an "active and influential agent of change".[2] To borrow an analogy, the mediator plays the role of the "writer, director, and one of the central characters" in a play.[3] He employs "various moves, or techniques to promote the success of the mediation".[4] In the course of the mediation process, the mediator alters the perceptions of parties by whittling away at their closely held beliefs until they become small distinct pieces that are more malleable and amenable to being shaped. Finally, by "gradually re-polarizing and merging the inner portions of the model with those surrounding them", the mediator is able to find that elusive agreement.

It is clear, therefore, that mediators exercise a measure of control and influence in laying down the ground rules, enforcing them, setting the agenda, reality-testing the parties and guiding them towards the final outcome. In doing so, mediators are imbued with the power to shape interests and their influence of parties, whether overtly or indirectly, can be termed manipulation.

III. How do I manipulate thee? Let me count the ways

A. *Manipulating the setting*

(1) Example 1

Imagine entering a mediation room as a party. You push open the doors and are greeted by the soothing sounds of the ocean. As you look around the room, your eyes take in the framed photos of the mediator's smiling children and his happy family plastered all over the walls. The mediator warmly welcomes you and beckons you to take a seat, pointing at a comfy-looking chair.

None of this was random. In fact, manipulation started the minute parties entered the mediation venue. The lighting and furniture arrangements, the comforting atmosphere and calming sounds and the pictures of the mediator's family all create the impression of a warm, cosy space — a venue in which parties feel safe and relaxed, and hence may become more receptive towards collaboration. Furthermore, the mediator's control of the physical seating arrangements, where he positions the parties in relation to himself and each other, are aspects that have been carefully managed to ensure a conducive environment for the mediation.

B. *Manipulating the process*

(1) Example 2

An estranged couple is at a mediation session. Having heard the opening statements of both parties, you (the mediator) have distilled their concerns to three key issues — the amount of maintenance, the division of matrimonial assets and the care and control of the child. Through your observation of the tone, demeanour and words used by the parties, you sense that underlying all these issues is a deep-seated resentment and hurt experienced by one party at the adultery of the other party. In passing, one party mentions that their child's teacher has observed several behavioural problems such as being distracted in class, procrastinating on assignments, periods of moodiness and a persistent defiance towards teachers.

(2) Example 2, Scenario A

While having remained largely silent, you see the child's developmental needs as a potential source of mutual concerns and possible agreement. You make the judgment that dwelling upon the adultery is of little use and destructive towards forward movement. You choose to focus on the problems surfaced by the child's behaviour and ask for more details about the child's infractions in school, reframing the worries of the parents as possible areas for cooperation.

When faced with attempts to return to the issue of the adultery in the form of repeat accusations and continued re-descriptions of the betrayal, you (having actively listened and summarised these accusations earlier) make the judgment that without stronger intervention, the party will continue to wallow in past indiscretions and such fixations prevents forward movement towards resolution.

Thus you respond, "I understand that it must be painful for what you have gone through (and here you summarise again). Having said that, are there any new concerns you wish to raise? Having heard the facts a few times, I feel that it is not a productive use of our limited time to go over them again. I am interested, however, in understanding the rationale for your child's behavioural problems and working them out with you. Shall we return to it?"

(3) Example 2, Scenario B

In this alternative scenario, you decide that the underlying issue of betrayal must be resolved for agreement to be reached on the other issues.

As you ask for more details about the betrayal, one party is visibly discomforted and ignores your question or tries to deflect it, saying "I don't think it would be necessary to go there." You make the judgment that settlement cannot be reached without settling this issue and say "I appreciate the efforts of both parties in coming here to seek a settlement but for that to happen, a frank and candid disclosure is necessary. Until we achieve that, I do not see any way of moving towards settlement."

The examples shown above demonstrate that the mediation process is fraught with manipulation. As the mediator is continually exposed to new sources of information, he/she revises the agenda and adapts his/her own road map on how to proceed, refocusing the parties attention as necessary.

In this instance, the mediator exerts control over the mediation process by either encouraging the discussion of certain topics to build common ground[5] (e.g., the child's behavioural issues) or keep certain topics off the table if she anticipates a clash of views and positions[6] (e.g., the details of the adultery). Depending on the mediator's own evaluation and judgment, the agenda he formulates will influence the way in which he manages the process to guide parties and direct them towards a particular series of solutions or options. Both the mediator's management of agenda-setting and his control of the process are manipulative techniques used in the mediation process.

C. Manipulating the parties (reframing, reality-testing and rewarding)

Apart from controlling the process, the mediator manipulates the parties directly. He or she reframes statements to smoothen and take the edge off incendiary meanings, uses strategies such as the meta-model to challenge attribution biases, repackage information in a way that facilitates communication, reality-tests clients to keep them focused on problem-solving and cheers parties on, rewarding positive behaviour such as honesty and candour while encouraging and urging greater participation.

These are but a few manipulative techniques commonly used by mediators. We will focus on one: it has been said that an ounce of framing is worth a pound of reframing. Effective framing has been characterised as a "genuine and thoughtful effort to change the ways in which conflict is presented in language".[7] Framing itself "entails shaping, focusing and organizing in order to examine and understand a particular problem and make sense of a cluster of issues".[8]

Typically, in their opening statements in a mediation, parties frame the dispute and the issues. The mediator then uses reframing to "alter the language used to describe the dispute".[9] By modifying the language used, the mediator reshapes the discourse and thus manipulates the "perceptions, and current frames of the behaviour, attitudes or issues in the dispute".[10]

Reframing is thus used to accomplish an "alternative social account of the conflict", allowing parties to reinterpret their circumstances, their counterpart's motivations and the range of possible solutions.[11] In his attempt to create "a single perception of the dispute from a shared point of view"[12] so as to facilitate constructive discussion, the mediator constantly manipulates what the parties say.

Manipulation enables a mediator to change the presentation of the problem and re-characterise the participants in his own words, fully cognizant that in doing so, his altered words then bear a different meaning as understood by the parties. This results in a problem that is hopefully less intractable and possibly more amenable to resolution than the initial one. Essentially, the mediator changes the story line and shifts the entire conflict paradigm through reframing, altering how the parties view themselves and the conflict.[13]

Interestingly, apart from manipulating what the parties say, the mediator also manipulates what he wants them to hear. For instance, a mediator can use the guise of seeking clarification to reframe the statement or demand as issued by one party for another party to hear. Managing what one party says and another hears is a further step taken in the manipulation of the conflict paradigm.

Another way in which manipulation can be brought to bear is the powerful tool of reality-testing. Simply put, a settlement in mediation can be achieved when, all things considered, parties decide that what they can accomplish from the mediation is better than their BATNA (Best Alternative to a Negotiated Agreement) or superior to litigation.

To reach this point, the mediator can reality-test parties in three distinct situations. The first situation is after a significant amount of effort (time, money and energy) has been invested in the mediation. By drawing this to the parties' attention, the mediator can highlight the potential loss of everything accomplished. The second is when an agreement seems to be on the verge of breaking down. Similarly the mediator can draw the parties' attention to the potential loss while contrasting it with the prospect of litigation (and its attendant costs in both time and expenses) in the event of mediation's failure. The third situation in which reality-testing can be used as a manipulative device is when "the map is not the territory it represents".[14] This is a situation where the "perceptions (the map) of the individual does not adequately represent reality or the truth (the territory)".[15] Reality-testing thus serves to align the map to the territory and these three situations in which reality-testing is used serves to direct the parties towards "focusing discussion, procedurally and substantively, toward settlement".[16]

IV. The mediator's paradox

In the process of mediation, mediators carry out numerous functions: establishing a framework for cooperative decision-making, promoting constructive communication, providing appropriate evaluations, empowering the parties, and ensuring a minimum level of process and outcome fairness.[17]

Throughout all these functions, it is submitted that absolute impartiality and neutrality on a mediator's part is nothing more than a myth — because it is both unfeasible and impossible for mediators not to manipulate in a mediation.

From the very start of the parties' opening statement, the mediator (whether consciously or subconsciously) starts to evaluate and assess the implications of what he is hearing. He starts comparing the stories, filing away potential leads which he deems helpful, discarding possible problematic avenues and formulating potential solutions. This thought process continually requires the mediator to exercise his judgment and contour the strategies he devises in the mediation process.

This thought process leads to a manipulation of the process and the parties as argued earlier. Mediators influence the outcome by affecting the legitimacy of each party's point of view through their interventions, determination of the order of speaking, caucusing and reframing of parties' statements.[18]

Herein lies the mediator's paradox. On the one hand, it is recognised that pressuring parties to settle implicitly interferes with the paramount value of mediation — that of respecting parties' autonomy and encouraging self-determination.

On the other hand, the reality of mediation reveals that the mediator's effective fulfilment of his role inevitably involves the employment of certain techniques or strategies that manipulate the parties towards an end-point.

Given that manipulation is a given in mediation, two questions emerge. First, how and where do we draw a line between acceptable and unacceptable degrees of manipulation? Second, in light of the challenges and ethical choices faced by a mediator, how can a mediator maintain this delicate balance?

A. *What is manipulation? I know it when I see it*

In trying to find a criterion for distinguishing between acceptable and unacceptable degrees of manipulation, this author keeps returning to United States Supreme Court Justice Potter Stewart's threshold test for obscenity — I know it when I see it.

Being able to clearly demarcate a boundary, however, proves more difficult. Yet thinking about where to draw the line between what is acceptable and what is not is perhaps not the right question to ask. Ultimately, the use of manipulation on different parties gives rise to very different results. A mediator can do the exact same thing to two different parties and end up with dramatically different responses. These differences arise in part because of the parties' relationship with the mediator. Has rapport and trust been established? Does the party feel that the mediator understands and empathises with him or her? Has the interaction thus far been stifled or easy-going?

The answer to these questions gives us an insight into the parties' perception of their relationship with the mediator. This then informs their perception of his manipulation — the techniques described earlier may be considered intrusive and belittling by some or reassuring and supportive by others. Thus, the deciding factor we should focus on is the actual effect of the manipulation on party autonomy.

Party autonomy has been presented and described as "a space that ought not to be touched, a kind of special ground that should be left alone or even enlarged".[19] Manipulation is thus perceived as a violation of that static space. Another author describes autonomy as a dynamic space — "a large, three-dimensional shape, malleable in part, rigid in part, and endowed with an internal structure and vitality. When pressure is applied, it may yield, resist, or push back."[20]

Both dynamic and static pictures are not that different in that both see party autonomy as a clearly defined zone. Yet while the static conception zealously guards this zone, a dynamic conception recognises that party autonomy is a sensitive entity — it is flexible to the constraints and limitations of reality (time, energy, money and others). Just as how an un-manipulative mediator is a myth, so too is absolute and unfettered party autonomy. A decision made in the presence or due to the presence of manipulation does not by itself mean that autonomy is invaded. In an ideal situation, it will however mean that a conscious decision was made to forgo and constrain some degree of autonomy for an end result.

B. What should a mediator do?

The difficulty in trying to circumscribe mediator conduct through statutes, court rules and ethical codes is that mediation itself, much less manipulation, is too subtle and nuanced to be restricted by the letter of the law. The presence of model codes and ethical guidelines is in itself ineffectual insofar as these codes and guidelines are couched in general terms and fail to offer concrete examples demonstrating how a mediator should behave.

Returning to the earlier "ideal situation" —it is submitted that the best way a mediator can respect a party's self-determination and autonomy is to recognise situations in which the mediator himself, through manipulation, has subjected the party's autonomy to an uneasy pressure. Instead of thinking in terms of acceptable boundaries for manipulation, the sole criterion for determining when manipulation is excessive is when the mediator identifies clues that a party's autonomy is uneasily compromised.

Understanding how a party feels about the manipulative pressure applied can be seen in the following manifestations. Does a party seem reluctant or non-committal? Does he question or disagree with the reframe? Does he reject a line of questioning? Does she refuse or say no to a reality-test? These rejections of manipulation suggest that parties may perceive the mediator as imposing his/her own agenda or frames on the parties, signalling that party autonomy is under threat and self-determination undermined — hinting to the mediator that a step back is necessary.

It is of paramount importance that a mediator both identifies such a hint and acknowledges it by providing space for the parties to reclaim their own autonomy. Yet having said that, it is submitted that it may be impracticable for a mediator to consciously check his manipulation because some degree of stubbornness and reticence is expected of parties in a mediation. Similarly, diminishing the use of manipulative techniques simply because some resistance is encountered cannot be the way to go. This author endorses a dramatic step[21] where the mediator feels that party autonomy in the mediation has been compromised to a potentially significant degree. Assuming agreement has been reached, a mediator should stop the process prior to finalisation and impose a 24-hour cooling off period for parties to reflect on the agreement before signature. In the event that doubts surface, the parties are free to reconvene to explore these in greater depth.

V. *Quis custodiet ipsos custodes*? — Who will guard the guards themselves?

At this point, this author's conception of party autonomy as the determining criterion by which manipulation should be constrained may seem both overly simplistic and fraught with difficulties. First and foremost is the danger of having mediators themselves recognise instances of their manipulation and bear the responsibility of tempering their manipulation — a situation in which we allow the foxes to guard the chicken coop.

Yet while naïve and simplistic, this author believes in the following truths. First, parties seek the help of mediators to solve problems they could not resolve between themselves. Second, the approach of mediators is to help them move towards settlement and manipulation is an integral part of that craft. Third, respecting parties' autonomy means that we assume that they expect such pressure and are capable and willing to accept it to a degree. Fourth, that being said, mediators must remain vigilant to the possibility of an overwhelming invasion into party autonomy and offer exit routes for parties to regain their own autonomy.

The problem of manipulation in mediation is indeed "not one well suited to simple line drawing or name calling",[22] because the acceptability of manipulative techniques varies as between parties and mediators. However, ethical mediation requires a balancing of alternative courses of manipulative action in a mediation and a judgment call as to how far a mediator can go to achieve the end-results while respecting the underlying values of mediation. At the end of the day when all is said and done, a mediator's discretion in making such judgment calls must be guided by his commitment to the spirit of the law and his respect for the integrity of the mediation process.

Endnotes

1. Oxford Dictionaries Website <http://www.oxforddictionaries.com/definition/english/manipulation> (accessed 23 October 2015).
2. Catherine Morris, "The Trusted Mediator: Ethics and Interaction in Mediation", in *Rethinking Disputes: The Mediation Alternative* (Julie Macfarlane ed.) (Toronto: Emond Montgomery, 1997) at 347.
3. Gary Smith, "Unwilling Actors: Why Voluntary Mediation Works, Why Mandatory Mediation Might Not" (1998) 36 *Osgoode Hall Law Journal* 847 ("*Smith*").
4. *Smith*, see above note 3 at 849 and 861.
5. Arghavan Gerami, "Bridging the theory-and-practice gap: Mediator power in practice" (2009) 26 *Conflict Resolution Quarterly* 433 ("*Gerami*") at 441.
6. *Gerami,* see above note 5 at 442.
7. Julie Macfarlane, "Mediating Ethically: The Limits of Codes of Conduct and a Potential of a Reflective Practice" (2002) 40 *Osgoode Hall Law Journal* 49.
8. *Gerami*, see above note 5 at 442.
9. *Smith*, see above note 3 at 859.

10. Christopher N. Candlin & Yon Maley, "Framing the Dispute" (1994) 7 *International Journal of Semiotics* 75.

11. Barbara Gray, "Mediation as Framing and Framing within Mediation" in *The Blackwell Handbook of Mediation: Bridging Theory, Research, and Practice* (Margaret S. Herrman ed.) (Blackwell, 2006).

12. *Smith,* see above note 3 at 859.

13. Bernard S. Mayer, *The Dynamics of Conflict Resolution*: *A Practitioner's Guide* (San Francisco: Jossey-Bass, 2000) at 383.

14. Alfred Korzypski, *Science and Sanity: An Introduction to Non-Aristotelian Systems and General Semantics* (Lakeville, Conn: International Non-Aristotelian Library Pub. Co., 1958) at 58–60.

15. Joel Lee, "Overcoming Attribution Bias in Mediation: An NLP Perspective" (2004) 15(1) *Australian Dispute Resolution Journal* 48 at 49.

16. Susan S. Silbey & Sally E. Merry, "Mediator Settlement Strategies", in *Mediation: Theory, Policy and Practice* (Carrie Menkel-Meadow ed.) (Aldershot: Ashgate Publishing, 2001).

17. Laurence Boulle & Kathleen J. Kelly, *Mediation: Principles, Process, Practice* (Toronto: Butterworths, 1998).

18. Rex M. Fuller, William D. Kimsey & Bruce C. McKinney, "Mediator Neutrality and Storytelling Order" (1992) 10(2) *Mediation Quarterly* 187.

19. David E. Matz, "Mediator Pressure and Party Autonomy: Are They Consistent with Each Other?" (1994) 10 *Negotiation Journal* 359 ("*Matz*").

20. *Matz,* see above note 19 at 363.

21. Proposal by *Matz,* see above note 19.

22. *Matz,* see above note 19.

The SIAC–SIMC Arb–Med–Arb Protocol: Enforcing International Commercial Mediated Settlement Agreements (MSAs) through the New York Convention

By Chng Teck Kian Desmond

I. Introduction

Arbitration remains the most popular means to resolve international commercial disputes and there is increasing interest in international commercial meditation.[1] Yet, there remains some amount of uncertainty regarding the cross-border enforceability of MSAs.[2]

Mediated settlement agreements ("MSAs")[3] do not intrinsically lend themselves to enforcement by the courts.[4] The UNCITRAL Model Law on Conciliation provides that MSAs are binding and enforceable but does not prescribe any enforcement procedure.[5] Currently, MSA enforcement relies on contract law, court consent decrees or consent arbitral awards — all of which have not proved completely satisfactory.[6]

While parties generally comply with MSAs,[7] a credible enforcement mechanism for cross-border MSA enforcement remains crucial in promoting international commercial mediation[8] by bolstering greater confidence in the mediation process and outcome.[9] Even those most optimistic about mediation cannot say that MSAs are *always* complied with.[10] Enforcement provides an added inducement for compliance,[11] and secures mediated outcomes on the off chance of non-compliance.[12]

The SIAC–SIMC Arb–Med–Arb is the first institutionalised arb–med–arb process that integrates the services of the Singapore International

Arbitration Centre ("SIAC") and the Singapore International Mediation Centre ("SIMC") to facilitate cross-border enforcement of MSAs through the New York Convention ("NYC").[13]

II. The SIAC–SIMC Arb–Med–Arb protocol & the New York convention

The SIAC–SIMC Arb–Med–Arb facilitates cross-border enforcement of MSAs by recording them as consent awards[14] to be enforced under the widely subscribed the NYC.[15] The procedure starts by initiating arbitration proceedings at the SIAC,[16] which are then stayed while mediation is conducted at the SIMC.[17] If the dispute is not settled, arbitration proceedings resume.[18] If the dispute is settled,[19] parties may request the tribunal to record the MSA as a consent award.[20]

A. *Enforcing contractual outcomes under the NYC*

The NYC allows refusal of enforcement if the award has not yet become "binding on the parties".[21] In determining if procedures "akin to arbitration" could produce contractual outcomes enforceable under the NYC, Italian courts recognised binding contracts as sufficiently binding, but German courts disagreed for contracts to remain subject to be reviewed on their merits under contract law.[22] The consensus now is that procedures "akin to arbitration" are not enforceable under the NYC.[23]

The SIAC–SIMC Arb–Med–Arb engages the arbitration process and is not merely a procedure "akin to arbitration". The outcome is a consent award that is just as binding as an arbitral award enforceable under the NYC.[24] However, MSAs with conditional terms would not be sufficiently binding.[25]

B. *Overcoming "differences": Invoking the arbitration jurisdiction*

The SIAC–SIMC Arb–Med–Arb is not the first attempt at enforcement of MSAs through the NYC. The Stockholm Chamber of Commerce

Mediation Rules 2014 ("SCC Mediation Rules") provides for the "med–arb" procedure, where parties begin with mediation and, upon settlement, appoint the mediator to be arbitrator in order to confirm the MSA as an arbitral award.[26] There is much debate over whether such a med–arb award is enforceable under the NYC,[27] although the weight seems to fall in the negative because a settlement would resolve any dispute necessary to invoke the tribunal's jurisdiction.[28]

The NYC only applies to agreements submitting "differences" to arbitration,[29] and provides for the recognition and enforcement of arbitral awards "arising out of differences between persons".[30] Most arbitration laws define arbitration agreement as an agreement to submit "disputes" or "controversies" to arbitration.[31] Moreover, a mediated settlement cannot amount to a "difference" that is "capable of settlement by arbitration" and is not enforceable according to art V(2)(a).[32]

However, the NYC does not stipulate when the "difference" has to exist in relation to the arbitration agreement.[33] Moreover, parties may have intended for settlement to be pre-conditioned by its recording as an arbitral award. Also, mediated outcomes might not necessarily involve admission of liability and so a legal dispute continues to exist.[34]

The SIAC–SIMC Arb–Med–Arb avoids this problem by initiating arbitration proceedings before mediation, eliminating any doubt regarding the arbitration agreement's validity. Mediation begins after the exchange of notice and response to arbitration.[35] This is sufficient to amount to a dispute because a dispute requires only an assertion or claim of a legal entitlement and the denial by the counter-party.[36]

Some say that mediation should occur only after the parties have made their submissions to the tribunal so parties would be "softened up by the preparation".[37] Under the SIAC–SIMC Arb–Med–Arb, the notice and response of arbitration are brief.[38] However, this does not mean that the parties will be ill prepared for settlement. Facilitative mediation similarly presents the opportunity for opening statements and agenda setting.[39] The mediator may also use reality-testing techniques to get parties to determine their relative strengths. Furthermore, too much emphasis on the legal case may entrench the rights-based paradigm and impede interests-based mediation. Starting mediation early is also more time and cost effective.[40]

C. *Enforcing consent awards under the New York convention*

Many arbitration institutes (including the SIAC[41]) have rules facilitating consent awards.[42] The UNCITRAL Model Law on International Commercial Arbitration ("Model Law (Arb)") provides for a settlement by parties to be recorded as an "award on agreed terms", which has the "same status and effect as any other award".[43] However, the NYC only mentions "arbitral awards" — without reference to consent awards.[44] This raises the issue of whether consent awards are enforceable as arbitral awards under the NYC.[45]

There may also be a further distinction between jurisdictions that adopt the Model Law (Arb)'s "same status and effect" wording, and others that recognise consent awards as arbitral awards.[46] Some argue that consent awards enjoying "same status and effect" do so only under domestic law, and are not technically "arbitral awards" enforceable under the NYC.[47]

However, such a distinction may be "pure semantics" and would be contrary to the NYC preference for international consistency.[48] Moreover, since the purpose of the Model Law (Arb) settlement provision is to promote settlement,[49] it should be interpreted in a way that would facilitate MSA settlement to further this purpose. For certainty, arbitration laws might adopt wording that explicitly recognises consent awards as arbitral awards.

Yet, the objection remains that the NYC was never intended to include consent awards.[50] Hence, there may be no treaty obligation to recognise consent awards. Nevertheless, given that many jurisdictions and arbitration institutes provide for consent awards as arbitral awards,[51] and given the recent efforts to further promote settlement[52] to address the increasing arbitration costs,[53] it is unlikely this would pose too much of an obstacle. Moreover, academic consensus is that consent awards are enforceable under the NYC.[54]

III. Mediation and arbitration: An imperfect fit

The integration of mediation and arbitration has been hailed as "the best of both worlds".[55] Hence, the hybrid med–arb process is promoted as an efficient and cost-effective[56] procedure that maintains party autonomy in mediation,[57] while providing the certainty of an arbitration outcome.[58] Some believe parties are more likely to settle in med–arb for fear of losing self-determination in arbitration.[59] Parties resolve complex interrelated issues in a holistic, value-creating manner during the mediation phase.[60] Even if not all issues are successfully mediated, med–arb can reduce the issues that go to arbitration.[61] Naturally, arb–med–arb provides these same benefits.

However, med–arb is not without drawbacks.[62] The main criticism is that interests-based mediation and rights-based arbitration[63] are inherently incompatible.[64]

A. *Have your cake and eat it too? Due process and confidentiality*

While settlement is common in arbitrations,[65] settlement negotiations focusing on relative legal merits[66] are different from facilitative mediations exploring broader extra-legal interests.[67] Confidentiality is vital to mediation if parties are to openly share information and interests in engendering creative, mutually beneficial and value-added outcomes.[68] Yet, due process is paramount in arbitration because it is a determinative process that is generally non-appealable.[69] These are competing values that result in inevitable trade-offs.[70]

Most of the concerns result from having the same neutral as mediator that later becomes arbitrator in "med–arb (same)".[71] While this saves time and cost,[72] it leads to behavioural and due process problems.[73] However, even if different neutrals are used in "med–arb (diff)",[74] some problems remain.[75]

The Singapore International Arbitration Act ("IAA") empowers arbitrators to also act as mediators,[76] while the SIAC–SIMC Arb–Med–Arb Protocol, SIMC Rules and the SIAC Rules do not prohibit the use of the same neutral.[77] However, the SIMC has indicated that different neutrals will generally be appointed in the arb–med–arb process, unless parties otherwise agree.[78] Since the above concerns equally apply to arb–med–arb,[79] parties should insist on having different neutrals.[80]

(1) *Problems in med–arb (same)*

(a) Affecting arbitration

Integrating mediation into the arbitration regime may expose the arbitral award to challenges for breach of natural justice.[81] While Singapore courts have rejected the UK "substantial injustice" approach,[82] judicial intervention for breach of natural justice remains somewhat restrained given the requirement to identify the specific natural justice rule,[83] and to prove actual prejudice.[84] The two pillars of natural justice are that the adjudicator must be unbiased, and must provide parties a fair hearing.[85]

(i) Treating parties in a discriminatory fashion:
     Mediator-arbitrator bias

Courts have found breach of natural justice where parties were not treated equally due to arbitrator bias.[86] Mediators are expected to be neutral,[87] but the mediator-arbitrator cannot be completely neutral in arbitration due to information received in mediation.[88] Since relevant facts in mediation differ from arbitration,[89] mediator-arbitrators must disregard prejudicial information that should not influence his decision as arbitrator,[90] or would not otherwise surface in arbitration.[91]

Also, reality-testing by the mediator-arbitrator may be perceived as a pre-determination of the arbitration outcome.[92] Suggestions made by mediator-arbitrators in brainstorming sessions or evaluative mediation may similarly suggest bias.[93] Asking even-handed questions[94] or refraining from making suggestions may overcome this. Yet, making recommendations is characteristic of evaluative mediation,[95] and parties sometimes seek this guidance.[96]

Impartiality may be demonstrated through well-reasoned awards based on fact and law.[97] Moreover, judges and jurors are similarly asked to disregard prejudicial evidence.[98] Nonetheless, some remain sceptical of the human ability to disregard prejudice.[99] Mediator-Arbitrators should be prudent in acknowledging this potential bias while assuring parties of their efforts to be impartial.[100]

(ii) Denying party's right to reply: Private sessions

There is breach of natural justice when a party is denied equal treatment in presenting his case.[101] This may include the civil law principle prohibiting the admissibility of evidence unless the other party has had the opportunity to comment or contradict.[102] Hence, it may be objectionable for a mediator-arbitrator to rely on information received during private sessions because the other party would not have the opportunity to respond.[103]

However, S17(3) of the IAA requires mediator-arbitrators to disclose any confidential information gathered during mediation that they consider material to the arbitration before arbitration resumes,[104] which allows parties the opportunity to respond.[105] Nonetheless, mediator-arbitrators should address their use of the confidential information in their mediation opening statement.[106]

(iii) Apparent bias

There may be apparent bias when mediator-arbitrators use private sessions, reality-testing[107] or suggest options.[108] However, apparent bias would not generally render an award vulnerable because of the Singapore requirement to prove actual prejudice[109] — although other courts may be different.[110]

(iv) Curing due process irregularities & public policy

Parties may agree not to challenge the award based on the role of the mediator-arbitrator.[111] Moreover, parties' consent to the use of confidential information may avoid compromising the arbitration.[112] There may also be waiver of due process rights by signature to the consent award.[113]

However, courts may nevertheless refuse recognising due process breaches on public policy grounds.[114] Also, due process rights may be unwaivable.[115] Nonetheless, it is likely that courts would similarly require proof of actual prejudice and not set-aside awards for apparent bias.

(b) Affecting mediation

The prospect of subsequent arbitration and confidentiality issues arising from the possibility of contractual enforcement of the MSA may detrimentally affect parties' behaviour in mediation.[116] While many of these issues may be overcome by facilitative mediation,[117] they make the mediator's job harder.

(i) Private sessions

Private sessions are critical to the exploration of interests and options, and reality-testing in mediation.[118] However, due process concerns in arbitration have led some to discourage private sessions unless with clear consent,[119] or even avoid mediation's "most significant feature"[120] altogether.[121] Moreover, given the primacy of privacy in private sessions, the possibility of confidential information being subsequently disclosed undermines the effectiveness of private sessions.[122]

(ii) Collaboration

Collaboration is conducive for agreement.[123] While the SIMC mediators may use varying styles,[124] the SIMC[125] provides training for facilitative mediation,[126] which involves collaborative problem-solving.[127] However, parties may be tempted to be adversarial and seek to influence a mediator-arbitrator to gain an advantage in arbitration.[128] Given that material confidential information may be disclosed in arbitration,[129] parties may exploit private sessions to unilaterally undermine the other party's case,[130] or pre-emptively make their case in an "early trial run".[131] Even with disclosure, the other party may be caught off guard.[132] Even if the information is not material, it may still influence the mediator-arbitrator.[133]

(iii) Open communication

Open communication is vital for exploration of interests, brainstorming, correcting information asymmetries and reality-testing.[134] However, parties may be more reticent in sharing information with a mediator-arbitrator.[135] This impedes the accurate understanding of interests necessary for mutually acceptable arrangements.[136]

However, others contend that there will always be some distrust among disputing parties and it is up to the mediator to skilfully alleviate these concerns.[137] Moreover, the presence of the mediator-arbitrator may encourage parties to take mediation more seriously.[138] Furthermore, parties may be more willing to confide in the mediator-arbitrator "precisely because he may ultimately decide their fate".[139]

(iv) Consensuality of outcomes

Consensuality is perhaps the defining characteristic of mediation.[140] Party autonomy in controlling the final outcome[141] ensures party satisfaction. However, the presence of a mediator-arbitrator may result in coercive pressure for parties to settle on terms suggested by the potential arbitrator.[142] Mediator-arbitrators may be tempted to use "the gentle threat" of an unfavourable decision to induce settlement.[143] Such strong-arm tactics undermine the legitimacy of mediation because parties feel excluded from the process,[144] and reduce satisfaction with — and commitment to — the mediated outcome that parties perceive as imposed.[145] However, this danger exists even in traditional mediation,[146] and a facilitative mediator should be able to diffuse any potential coercive pressure.[147]

(2) Problems in med–arb (diff)

(a) Affecting mediation

(i) Collaboration

The prospect of a subsequent arbitration may tempt parties to pre-emptively posture themselves as adversaries.[148] If parties treat the mediation merely as prelude to arbitration,[149] facilitative mediation would be more challenging. However, this may not be too problematic because parties choosing arb–med–arb are concerned with the enforceability of mediated settlements, suggesting that they genuinely want to mediate.

(ii) Open communication: Confidentiality

The prospect of subsequent arbitration may cause parties to be less candid. This is because complete confidentiality in mediation is "illusory".[150] Even though mediation is "without prejudice",[151] the inadmissible information may nonetheless be used strategically.[152] Moreover, public policy exceptions to "without prejudice" mean that there is no guarantee of confidentiality.[153] "Without prejudice" communication may be admitted in subsequent legal proceedings to prove the existence of the MSA,[154] construe the MSA terms,[155] prove misrepresentation, fraud or undue influence,[156] or any other unambiguous impropriety.[157] The SIAC Rules allow for disclosure in enforcing an award or legal right.[158] However, parties may be prevented from using the confidential information because the SIMC Rules prohibit any disclosure unless "required by applicable law",[159] such as a subpoena.[160]

Confidentiality is even more uncertain in relation to subsequent arbitration. Arbitration tribunals are often pragmatic in establishing the facts rather than applying technical evidential rules.[161] Hence, they may be more willing to admit "without prejudice" communication.

However, arbitrators in the institutionalised SIAC–SIMC Arb–Med–Arb procedure may be more inclined to exclude "without prejudice" communication to preserve the integrity of the mediation process. The SIAC may consider enacting stricter "without prejudice" rules specific to arb–med–arb. In any case, parties may agree not to introduce information that is not independently discoverable.[162]

B. Ill-fitting hook: Arbitration regime unable to fully accommodate mediation

Since the NYC was not designed to integrate mediation, utilising the arbitration regime to enforce MSAs is a "convenient" but "ill-fitting hook".[163] Rights-based remedies in arbitration may not fully enforce creative, interest-based mediated outcomes. Also, arbitration grounds for non-enforcement do not adequately protect mediation parties.

(1) Unable to fully enforce mediated outcomes

Mediated outcomes often eschew orthodox rights and duties in favour of "future-focused and contingent" solutions that meet the interests of all parties.[164] Mediators may reframe a dispute in a de-legalising and de-monetising way to facilitate the mediation process.[165] The legalised remedies of rights-based systems, such as arbitration, may not accommodate these outcomes.[166] Moreover, conditional outcomes would not be sufficiently binding for NYC enforcement.[167]

Outcomes involving new business relationships[168] may be outside the arbitral mandate.[169] Also, arbitration agreements may exclude certain remedies, restricting the range of meditated outcomes.[170] Nevertheless, the arbitral mandate may be extended by explicit agreement,[171] or implied consent.[172]

However, parties may expressly empower the tribunal to decide as *amiables compositeur*, or *ex eaquo et bono*.[173] While the scope of this discretion is unsettled,[174] the idea is that arbitrators would be entitled to depart from the strictures of the law based on their own notions of justice,[175] subject to mandatory rules and public policy.[176] This may include considerations of equity, commercial usages, and the arbitrator's conscience producing an "equitable and acceptable solution" that adapts the law[177] or alters the contract.[178] This "less 'legalistic' approach"[179] may suit mediated consent awards.[180]

The reliance on litigation and arbitration for enforcement could discourage the "depth, creativity and richness" of mediated outcomes.[181] Perhaps some outcomes can only depend on efforts to encourage compliance.

(2) Unable to adequately protect parties to mediation

While the NYC provides for settlement, it is not designed for mediation.[182] Hence, the NYC grounds for non-enforcement may provide insufficient protection.[183] Mediation does not have strict procedural and discovery rules because parties retain control over the outcome, which are then contractually enforceable — subject to undue influence, coercion, fraud, mistake and frustration.[184] However, NYC does not provide the same protections to arbitral awards, which become enforceable even if the MSA is not contractually enforceable.[185] This leaves parties to mediation without remedy.[186] Moreover, further modifications may be needed to account for mediator and counsel misconduct.[187]

IV. Conclusion

Given that arb–med–arb is motivated by enforcement of mediated outcomes,[188] the rules should perhaps favour mediation values. Yet, doing so might risk non-recognition under the NYC arbitration regime. Since neither arbitration nor contract laws are completely suitable for mediation,[189] a bespoke international convention on MSA enforcement may be most ideal.[190]

Until then, the SIAC–SIMC Arb–Med–Arb may be the best bet for cross-border MSA enforcement. One suggestion might be to expressly allow parties to opt out of the arbitration after the mediation phase if they feel the arbitration would be compromised.[191] The SIAC–SIMC Arb–Med–Arb Protocol envisages mandatory arbitration if parties do not settle.[192] Presently, arbitration proceedings may only be terminated by mutual consent,[193] although they may challenge an impartial arbitrator after the mediation phase.[194] The option to opt out might encourage parties to be more collaborative in mediation. Moreover, the current procedure may deter parties who desire mediation but not arbitration.[195]

Endnotes

1. Even in high-value commercial disputes. Andrew Phang, "Alternative Dispute Resolution and Regional Prosperity — A View from Singapore" (Address delivered at the China–ASEAN Justice Forum in September 2014) <https://www.supremecourt.gov.sg/data/doc/ManagePage/5522/China-ASEAN%20Justice%20Forum%20-%20ADR%20and%20Regional%20Prosperity%20(Final)%2011092014%20(Phang%20JA)%20highlighted.pdf> (accessed 7 November 2015) at [10] and [14]; S. I. Strong, "Beyond International Commercial Arbitration? The Promise of International Commercial Mediation" (2014) 45 *Washington University Journal of Law & Policy* 10 (*"Strong"*) at 11 and 14; Bobette Wolski, "Arb-Med-Arb (and MSAs): A Whole Which is Less Than, Not Greater Than, the Sum of Its Parts?" (2013) 6 *Contemporary Asia Arbitration Journal* 249 (*"Wolski 2013"*) at 253 and 255.

2. *Wolski 2013*, see above note 1 at 255.

3. Mediated Settlement Agreements refer to agreements reached as an outcome of mediation; Bobette Wolski, "Enforcing Mediated Settlement Agreements (MSAs): Critical Questions and Directions for Future Research" (2014) 7 *Contemporary Asia Arbitration Journal* 87 (*"Wolski 2014"*) at 89.

4. Since commercial mediation occurs outside the court system; *Wolski 2013*, see above note 1 at 256.

5. United Nations Commission on International Trade Law (UNCITRAL) Model Law on International Commercial Conciliation (19 November 2002), Art 14; Brette L Steele, "Enforcing International Commercial Mediation Agreements as Arbitral Awards under the New York Convention" (2006–2007) 54 *UCLA Law Review* 1385 (*"Steele"*) at 1387.

6. For a summary on these approaches, refer to *Wolski 2014*. See above note 3 at 93–99.

7. Laurence Boulle, "International Enforceability of Mediated Settlement Agreements: Developing the Conceptual Framework" (2014) 7(1) *Contemporary Asia Arbitration Journal* 35 (*"Boulle"*) at 40.

8. It has been noted that the uncertainty in enforcing MSAs contributes to the underutilisation of international commercial mediation; *Steele,* see above note 5 at 1392.

9. *Wolski 2014*, see above note 3 at 104.

10. *Strong*, see above note 1 at 35.

11. *Boulle*, see above note 7 at 57.

12. *Wolski 2014*, see above note 3 at 104.

13. Convention on the Recognition and Enforcement of Foreign Arbitral Awards (10 June 1958), 330 UNTS 3 (*"NYC"*); Christopher Boog & Elisabeth Leimbacher, "The Singapore International Mediation Centre and the new AMA Procedure — finally what users have always wanted?" Singapore International Mediation Centre <http://simc.com.sg/singapore-international-mediation-centre-new-ama-procedure-%EF%AC%81nally-users-always-wanted/> (accessed 7 November 2015) (*"Boog & Leimbacher"*).

14. Consent awards refer to settlement agreements rendered as awards; Jeffrey Waincymer, *Procedure and Evidence in International Arbitration* (The Hague: Kluwer Law International, 2012) (*"Waincymer"*) at 1283.

15. "SIAC–SIMC Arb–Med–Arb Protocol", Art 9, Singapore International Mediation Centre website <http://simc.com.sg/siac-simc-arb-med-arb-protocol/> (accessed 7 November 2015); *Steele*, see above note 5 at 1387.

16. SIAC–SIMC Arb–Med–Arb Protocol Art 2.

17. SIAC–SIMC Arb–Med–Arb Protocol Arts 5, 6.

18. SIAC–SIMC Arb–Med–Arb Protocol Art 8.

19. SIMC Rules require all mediated settlement agreements to be made in writing and signed by or on behalf of the parties; "SIMC Rules", R 8.1, Singapore International Mediation Centre website <http://simc.com.sg/mediation-rules/> (accessed 7 November 2015).

20. SIAC-SIMC Arb-Med-Arb Protocol Art 9.

21. *NYC* Art. V(1)(e); *Steele*, see above note 5 at 1394–1395.

22. Either internally within the rules of the dispute resolution process that is "akin to arbitration", or by an application to court; Steele, see above note 5 at 1395–1396; Nigel Blackaby & Constantine Partasides with Martin Hunter & Alan Redfern, *Redfern and Hunter on International Arbitration*

(New York: Oxford University Press, 5th Edition, 2009) (*"Redfern and Hunter"*) at [11.85].

23. *Steele*, see above note 5 at 1396.

24. Both the SIAC Rules and the Singapore IAA provide that the effect of an award is final and binding; "SIAC Rules", R 28.9, Singapore International Arbitration Centre website <http://www.siac.org.sg/our-rules/rules/siac-rules-2013> (accessed 7 November 2015); International Arbitration Act (Cap 143A, 2002 Rev. Ed.) ("IAA") s 19B(1).

25. Andrew Tweeddale & Keren Tweeddale, *Arbitration of Commercial Disputes: International and English Law and Practice* (New York: Oxford University Press, 2005) (*"Tweeddale"*) at [10.42].

26. These rules were first introduced in 2000; "SCC Mediation Rules", Art 14, Arbitration Institute of the Stockholm Chamber of Commerce website <http://sccinstitute.com/media/40123/mediationrules_eng_webbversion. pdf> (accessed 7 November 2015); Christopher Newark & Richard Hill, "Can a Mediated Settlement Become an Enforceable Arbitration Award?" (2000) 16 *Arbitration International* 81 (*"Newark & Hill"*) at 81.

27. Edna Sussman, "The New York Convention Through a Mediation Prism" (2008–2009) 15 *Dispute Resolution Magazine* 10 (*"Sussman"*) at 12; *Wolski 2014*, see above note 3 at 97.

28. Procedurally, it is argued that enforcement requires the supply of the arbitration agreement under Art II(1)(b) NYC and the failure to produce a valid arbitration agreement would prevent enforcement; *Wolski 2013*, see above note 1 at 262; *Newark & Hill*, see above note 26 at 83–84; Ronan Feehily, "The Legal Status and Enforceability of Mediated Settlement Agreements" (2013) 12 *Hibernian Law Journal* 1 (*"Feehily"*) at 21.

29. NYC Art II(1).

30. NYC Art I(1).

31. UNCITRAL Model Law on International Commercial Arbitration (21 June 1985) ("Model Law (Arb)"), Art 7(1); UK Arbitration Act 1996 (c 23)(UK) s 6(1); US Federal Arbitration Act 9 USC (US) § 1; IAA s 2A, see above note 24; Arbitration Ordinance (Cap 609) (Hong Kong) s 19; Gary B. Born, *International Commercial Arbitration* (The Hague: Kluwer Law International, 2nd Edition, 2014) (*"Born"*) at 338.

32. *Newark & Hill*, see above note 25 at 84.

33. *Sussman,* see above note 27 at 12. However, Art 30 Model Law (Arb) requires settlement to occur "during arbitral proceedings".

34. Some courts have held that a dispute remains unless there is unequivocal admission of both liability and quantum of claim; *Glencore Grain Ltd v*

Agros Trading Co [1999] 2 *Lloyd's Law Reports* 410 at [38]; *Tjong Very Sumito v Antig Investments* [2009] 4 *Singapore Law Reports (Reissue)* 732 at [64]; *Getwick Engineers Ltd v Pilecon Engineering Ltd* (2002) 1020 *Hong Kong Cases Unreported* 1 at [23(3)] following *Tai Hing Cotton Mill Ltd v Glencore Grain Rotterdam BV* [1996] 1 *Hong Kong Cases* 363 at [47] and cited with approval in *P T Tri-M G Intra Asia Airlines v Norse Air Charter Limited* [2009] Singapore High Court 13 at [58].

35. SIAC–SIMC Arb–Med–Arb Protocol Art 5.

36. *Born*, see above note 31 at 338.

37. Where the initiation of the arbitration is mere formality, parties may miss the opportunity to master the facts and delineate the issues — and overlook the "foundation" for future settlement such that "the case is not well framed"; Lon Fuller, "Collective Bargaining and the Arbitrator" (1963) *Wisconsin Law Review* 3 (*"Fuller"*) at 26; *Wolski 2013*, see above note 1 at 266.

38. SIAC Rules, R 3 & R 4.

39. *Steele,* see above note 5 at 1402; *Boulle,* see above note 7 at 49.

40. *Waincymer,* see above note 14 at 712.

41. SIAC Rules, R 28.8.

42. For examples, *Wolski 2014*, see above note 3 at 96, footnote 49; *Tweeddale,* see above note 25 at [10.42].

43. Model Law (Arb), Art 30.

44. NYC Art 1; Winnie Jo-Mei Ma, "Enforcing Mediated Settlement Agreemens under the New York Convention: From Controversies to Creativities? (2014) 7 *Contemporary Asia Arbitration Journal* 69 (*"Winnie"*) at 75; *Steele,* see above note 5 at 1397.

45. *Tweeddale,* see above note 25 at [10.42].

46. *Steele*, see above note 5 at 1397–1398.

47. *Steele*, see above note 5 at 1397–1398.

48. *Steele*, see above note 5 at 1398.

49. *Wolski 2014*, see above note 3 at 96; *Redfern and Hunter*, see above note 22 at [9.36].

50. Preparatory documents to the negotiations of the NYC suggest that NYC was not intended to cover consent awards because it was raised but not decided upon; "UNCITRAL Secretariat Guide on the Convention on the Recognition and Enforcement of Foreign Arbitral Awards", New York Convention 1958 website <http://newyorkconvention1958.org/pdf/Article%20I%20NYC%20-%20FINAL.pdf> (accessed 7 November 2015) at 12; *Travaux préparatoires*, Recognition and Enforcement of Foreign Arbitral

Awards, Report by the Secretary-General, Annex I, Comments by Governments, E/2822 at 7 and 10.

51. Pieter Sanders, "UNCITRAL's Model Law on International Commercial Conciliation" (2007) 23 Arb Int'l 105 at 139; *Wolski 2014*, see above note 3 at 96, footnote 49.

52. *Wolski 2014*, see above note 3 at 101.

53. Lucy Greenwood, "A Window of Opportunity? Building a Short Period of Time into Arbitral Rules in Order for Parties to Explore Settlement" (2011) 27 *Arbitration International* 199 ("*Greenwood*").

54. *Wolski 2013*, see above note 1 at 261.

55. Martin C. Weisman, "Med-Arb: The Best of Both Worlds" (Spring 2013) 19 (3) *Dispute Resolution Magazine* 40 ("*Weisman*"); Alan L Limbury, "Med-Arb: Getting the Best of Both Worlds" International Mediation Institute (29 February 2012) <https://imimediation.org/private/downloads/ MySABWewVWjL-3OWTf4eYg/hybrid-processes-2010---article-by-alan-limbury.pdf> (accessed 7 November 2015) ("*Limbury*").

56. Mark Batson Baril & Donald Dickey, "MED-ARB: The Best of Both Worlds or Just A Limited ADR Option?" Mediate.com website <http:// www.mediate.com/pdf/V2%20MED-ARB%20The%20Best%20of%20 Both%20Worlds%20or%20Just%20a%20Limited%20ADR%20Option. pdf> (accessed 7 November 2015) ("*Baril & Dickey*") at 4.

57. *Weisman*, see above note 55 at 40; *Limbury*, see above note 55 at 1.

58. *Limbury*, see above note 55 at 1–2; *Baril & Dickey*, see above note 56 at 4.

59. *Weisman*, see above note 55 at 40.

60. *Weisman*, see above note 55 at 41.

61. Parties may amend their claims under SIAC Rules, R 17.5; *Weisman*, see above note 55 at 41.

62. *Wolski 2013*, see above note 1 at 258.

63. *Boulle*, see above note 7 at 42.

64. *Fuller*, see above note 37 at 23; Sherry Landry, "Med-Arb: Mediation with a Bite and an Effective ADR Model" (1996) 63 *Defense Counsel Journal* 263 ("*Landry*") at 265.

65. *Wolski 2013*, see above note 1 at 268.

66. *Waincymer*, see above note 14 at p 715.

67. *Boulle*, see above note 7 at 49.

68. Jo-Anne Bigham, "Confidentiality and Without Prejudice: Illusory or Real?" (2006) 1 *Asian Journal on Mediation* 13 ("*Bigham*") at 15; Ellen E

Deason, "Procedural Rules for Complementary Systems of Litigation and Mediation — Worldwide" (2004–2005) 80 *Notre Dame Law Review* 553 at 563.

69. *Boulle*, see above note 7 at 42.

70. *Waincymer*, see above note 14 at 705.

71. For a description of the med–arb (same) process, *Wolski 2013,* see above note 1 at 259.

72. Using different neutrals would require extra time and effort in educating an additional neutral about the dispute. However, this may be offset by agreeing to the mediator narrowing the scope of the dispute through partial settlement and providing the arbitrator with an agreed list of remaining issues to be resolved by arbitration; *Wolski 2013,* see above note 1 at 258–260.

73. *Wolski 2013,* see above note 1 at 259 and 262.

74. For a description of the med–arb (different) process, *Wolski 2013,* see above note 1 at 258.

75. *Wolski 2013,* see above note 1 at 259.

76. IAA s 17(4) read with s 16(5)(a), see above note 24.

77. Except for the general conflict of interests and impartiality provisions SIMC Rules, Art 4.6; SIAC Rules, R 11.1.

78. "What is Arb-Med-Arb?" Singapore International Mediation Centre website <http://simc.com.sg/arb-med-arb/> (accessed 7 November 2015); *Boog & Leimbacher*, see above note 13 at 3.

79. *Wolski 2013*, see above note 1 at 262.

80. *Fuller*, see above note 37 at 23; *Wolski 2013*, see above note 1 at 260.

81. IAA s 24(b) "natural justice", see above note 24; Model Law (Arb) Art 34(1)(a)(ii) "unable to present his case"; *Greenwood*, see above note 53 at 207.

82. Under the UK approach, there must be "serious irregularity" giving rise to "substantial injustice" to warrant judicial intervention under breach of natural justice rules; UK Arbitration Act 1996 (c 23)(UK) s 68; *Lesotho Highlands Development Authority v Impregilo SpA* [2005] 2 *Lloyd's Law Reports* 310; Robert Merkin & Johanna Hjalmarsson, "Singapore Arbitration Legislation Annotated" (Informa, 2009) ("*Merkin & Hjalmarsson*") at 62–63.

83. *Merkin & Hjalmarsson,* see above note 82 at 63 citing *John Holland Pty Ltd v Toyo Engineering Corp (Japan)* [2001] 2 *Singapore Law Reports* 262.

84. *Merkin & Hjalmarsson,* see above note 82 at p 63 citing *Soh Beng Tee & Co Pte Ltd v Fairmont Development Pte Ltd* [2007] 3 *Singapore Law Reports* 86.

85. *Soh Beng Tee & Co Pte Ltd v Fairmont Development Pte Ltd* [2007] 3 *Singapore Law Reports* 86 at [43] citing *Gas & Fuel Corporation of Victoria v Wood Hall Ltd & Leonard Pipeline Contractors Ltd* [1978] VR 385 at 396.

86. *Merkin & Hjalmarsson,* see above note 82 at p 63 citing *Stockport Metropolitan Borough Council v O'Reilly* [1983] 2 *Lloyd's Law Reports* 70; *Rustal Trading SA v Gill & Duffus SA* [2000] 1 *Lloyd's Law Reports* 14; [2000] CLC 231 at 235.

87. Under SIMC Rules Art 4.5, mediators are expected to make a written declaration of their impartiality and independence, and disclose any known actual or potential conflicts of interests.

88. *Baril & Dickey,* see above note 56 at 5.

89. *Fuller,* see above note 37 at 24.

90. *Weisman,* see above note 55 at 41; *Fuller,* see above note 37 at 26; *Waincymer,* see above note 14 at 706.

91. *Waincymer,* see above note 14 at 711.

92. *Waincymer,* see above note 14 at 709–710; *Limbury,* see above note 55 at 3; Brian A. Pappas, "Med-Arb: The Best of Both Worlds May Be Too Good to Be True" (Spring 2013) 19 (3) *Dispute Resolution Magazine* 42 ("*Pappas*") at 43.

93. *Waincymer,* see above note 14 at pp 710–711.

94. *Limbury,* see above note 55 at 3; *Waincymer,* see above note 14 at 709–710.

95. *Boulle,* see above note 7 at 50.

96. *Waincymer,* see above note 14 at 708.

97. *Waincymer,* see above note 14 at 706.

98. *Landry,* see above note 64 at 265; *Weisman,* see above note 55 at 41; *Waincymer,* see above note 14 at 706.

99. This may be more so when evaluating the credibility of witness testimony in making findings of fact; *Pappas,* see above note 92 at 42; *Waincymer,* see above note 14 at 711.

100. *Weisman,* see above note 55 at 41.

101. NYC Art 36(1)(a)(ii); *Soh Beng Tee & Co Pte Ltd v Fairmont Development Pte Ltd* [2007] 3 *Singapore Law Reports* 86 at [42] (IAA s 22 "natural justice" has been held as substantively identical to Model Law (Arb) Art 18 "equal treatment of parties" in guaranteeing a "reasonable opportunity" to present one's case); *ADG v ADI* [2014] 3 *Singapore Law Reports* 481 at [118] (IAA s 22 "natural justice" is substantively the same as Art 34(2)

(a)(ii) non-recognition for inability to present case); *Merkin & Hjalmarsson*, see above note 82 at 63 citing *Re Fuerst Brothers Co Ltd and Stephenson* [1951] 1 *Lloyd's Law Reports* 429.

102. *Redfern and Hunter*, see above note 14 at [10.49].

103. *Pappas*, see above note 92 at 43; *Steele*, see above note 5 at 1403–1405.

104. While some have noted that IAA s 17(3) does not indicate how the confidential information can be used in the subsequent arbitration, it is clear that the premise of the section provides for the use of confidential information subject to disclosure; *Waincymer*, see above note 14 at 711.

105. IAA s 17(3) requires arbitrators acting as mediators to inform parties of any confidential information gathered during the mediation that they consider material to the arbitration; *Weisman*, see above note 55 at 41.

106. IAA s 17(3) requires arbitrators acting as mediators to inform parties of any confidential information gathered during the mediation that they consider material to the arbitration; *Weisman,* see above note 55 at 41.

107. *Baril & Dickey*, see above note 56 at 5; *Waincymer*, see above note 14 at 709.

108. *Baril & Dickey*, see above note 56 at 5.

109. *Merkin & Hjalmarsson*, see above note 82 at 63 citing *Soh Beng Tee & Co Pte Ltd v Fairmont Development Pte Ltd* [2007] 3 *Singapore Law Reports* 86.

110. While the UK Arbitration Act takes the stricter "substantial injustice" approach, UK cases relating to other adjudicatory regimes have held that apparent bias was sufficient to breach natural justice — including where the adjudicator had spoken to parties separately in an attempt at mediation; *Glencot Developments & Design Co Ltd v Ben Barrett and Son (Contractors) Ltd* [2011] *Building Law Reports* 207 at [20]–[21].

111. *Waincymer*, see above note 14 at p 706.

112. *Wolski 2013*, see above note 1 at 267.

113. *Steele,* see above note 5 at 1407.

114. Model Law (Arb) Art 34(2)(b)(ii) provides for the setting aside of awards on the basis of public policy. Public policy has been held to cover a wide variety of matters, including procedural matters; *Beijing Sinozonto Mining Investment Co Ltd v Goldenray Consortium (Singapore) Pte Ltd* [2014] 1 *Singapore Law Reports* 814 at [37]-[41]; *Merkin & Hjalmarsson*, see above note 82 at p 76; *Steele,* see above note 5 at 1407.

115. Due process rights may be unwaivable due to public policy; *Steele*, see above note 5 at 1407.

116. *Wolski 2013*, see above note 1 at 262.

117. *Waincymer*, see above note 14 at 707.

118. *Wolski 2013*, see above note 1 at 265; *Waincymer*, see above note 14 at 709; Ruth Charlton & Micheline Dewdney, *The Mediator's Handbook*, (Sydney: Lawbook Company, 2nd Edition, 2004) at p 93.

119. *Waincymer*, see above note 14 at pp 705 and 709.

120. *Wolski 2013*, see above note 1 at 265.

121. *Steele*, see above note 5 at 1405.

122. *Wolski 2013*, see above note 1 at 263.

123. Laurence Boulle, *Mediation: Principles, Process, Practice* (London: Butterworths, 3rd Edition, 2011) ("*Boulle 2011*") at [3.23].

124. "Who are the mediators on SIMC's panel?" Singapore International Mediation Centre website <http://simc.com.sg/resources/faqs/#mediators> (accessed 7 November 2015).

125. Singapore Mediation Centre.

126. Danny McFadden & George Lim, *Mediation in Singapore: A Practical Guide* (Singapore: Sweet & Maxwell, 2015) at [11.044].

127. *Boulle*, see above note 7 at 49.

128. *Pappas*, see above note 92 at 43.

129. IAA s 17(3), see above note 24.

130. *Pappas*, see above note 92 at 43–44.

131. *Wolski 2013*, see above note 1 at 259.

132. *Wolski 2013*, see above note 1 at 259.

133. *Wolski 2013*, see above note 1 at 260.

134. *Pappas*, see above note 92 at 42; *Limbury*, see above note 55 at 2.

135. *Pappas*, see above note 92 at 42; *Limbury,* see above note 55 at 2; *Waincymer*, see above note 14 at 711; *Greenwood*, see above note 53 at 207; Wayne D. Brazil, *Effective Approaches to Settlement* (Clifton, NJ: Prentice Hall Law & Business, 1988) ("*Brazil*") at 77.

136. *Brazil*, see above note 142 at 78.

137. *Brazil*, see above note 142 at 78.

138. For example, parties may "take the behavioural high road" to impress the mediator-arbitrator; *Brazil*, see above note 142 at 78.

139. One study concluded that with mediator-arbitrators, parties showed less hostility, were more actively brainstorming and generally more agreeable; *Landry*, see above note 64 at 265 and 267.

140. *Boulle 2011*, see above note 130 at [3.47].

141. *Boulle 2011*, see above note 130 at [3.40].

142. *Wolski 2013*, see above note 1 at 259; *Waincymer,* see above note 14 at 704.
143. *Fuller*, see above note 37 at 25; *Baril & Dickey*, see above note 56 at 4–5.
144. *Baril & Dickey*, see above note 56 at 5.
145. *Baril & Dickey*, see above note 56 at 5.
146. Boulle *2011*, see above note 130 at [3.47]–[3.48].
147. *Baril & Dickey*, see above note 56 at 5.
148. *Limbury*, see above note 55 at 3; *Pappas*, see above note 92 at 43.
149. *Limbury*, see above note 55 at 3.
150. *Bigham*, see above note 68 at 20.
151. "Without prejudice" is the common law protection of information exchanged in settlement negotiations by rendering them inadmissible in evidence; *Bigham*, see above note 68 at 16; *Ng Chuan Seng v Tan Ah Yoke* [1969] 2 *Malayan Law Journal* 75; *Ng Chee Weng v Lim Jit Ming Bryan* [2010] Singapore High Court 35.
152. Such as by assessing the relative weaknesses of parties' legal case; *Bigham*, see above note 68 at 17.
153. *Bigham*, see above note 68 at 14.
154. *Quek Kheng Leong Nicky v Teo Beng Ngoh* [2009] 4 *Singapore Law Reports (Reissue)* 181 at [24].
155. *Oceanbulk Shipping v TMT Asia* [2010] UK Supreme Court 44 at [40]–[41].
156. *Underwood v Cox* (1912) 4 *Dominion Law Reports* 66 cited in *Unilever PLC v The Procter & Gamble Co* [2000] 1 *Weekly Law Reports* 2436 at 2444 endorsed in *Quek Kheng Leong Nicky v Teo Beng Ngoh* [2009] 4 *Singapore Law Reports (Reissue)*181 at [23].
157. *Unilever PLC v The Procter & Gamble Co* [2000] 1 *Weekly Law Reports* 2436 at 2444 endorsed in *Quek Kheng Leong Nicky v Teo Beng Ngoh* [2009] 4 *Singapore Law Reports (Reissue)*181 at [23].
158. SIAC Rules, R 35.2.a & R 35.2.c.
159. SIMC Rules, R 9.2.
160. SIAC Rules, R 35.2.b provides for disclosure pursuant to a subpoena.
161. *Redfern and Hunter*, see above note 14 at [9.89].
162. *Waincymer*, see above note 14 at 705.
163. *Wolski 2014*, see above note 3 at 98; *Steele,* see above note 5 at 1412.
164. For example, agreements to use best efforts or even agreements to agree; *Boulle*, see above note 7 at 62.
165. *Boulle*, see above note 7 at 62.

166. Mediated outcomes not amenable to legal enforcement include use of best endeavours, conditional agreements and agreements to agree; *Boulle,* see above note 7 at 62.

167. *Tweeddale,* see above note 25 at [10.42].

168. *Steele,* see above note 5 at 1405.

169. NYC Art V(1)(c) provides for non-recognition of awards relating to disputes not contemplated by the submission to arbitration. *Steele,* see above note 5 at 1406.

170. *Waincymer,* see above note 14 at 713.

171. *Steele,* see above note 5 at 1406.

172. *Waincymer,* see above note 14 at 1284.

173. SIAC Rules, R 27.2.

174. Some argue that the doctrine must necessarily go beyond the conventional equitable principles, while others contend that it does not go so far as to modify the economics or the agreement; Sundaresh Menon *et al., Arbitration in Singapore: A Practical Guide* (Singapore: Sweet & Maxwell/Thomson Reuters, 2014) (*"Menon"*) at [6.119] and [6.122].

175. Hong-Lin Yu, "Amiable Composition — A Learning Curve" (2000) 17 *Journal of International Arbitration* 79 (*"Hong"*) at 81, 89–94 citing *Jager v Tolme and Runge* [1916] 1 KB 939; *Board of Trade v Cayzer Irvine & Co* [1927] AC 610.

176. *Hong,* see above note 182 at 84.

177. *Hong,* see above note 182 at 86.

178. *Hong,* see above note 182 at 81.

179. *Menon,* see above note 181 at [6.120].

180. *Amiables compositeurs* has its roots in the Code Napoleon and was intended to restore harmony between parties and to work out a new kind of legal relationship between them; *Hong,* see above note 182 at 79.

181. *Boulle,* see above note 7 at 63.

182. *Wolski 2013,* see above note 1 at 268; *Wolksi 2014,* see above note 3 at 99; *Winnie,* see above note 44 at 80.

183. *Wolski 2014,* see above note 3 at 98–99; *Winnie,* see above note 44 at 82.

184. *Feehily,* see above note 28 at 10–16; Catherine Cover Payne, "Enforceability of Mediated Agreements" (1985–1986) 1 *Ohio State Journal on Dispute Resolution* 385 at 388–396.

185. Although an argument may be made for non-recognition on the grounds of public policy under NYC Art V(2)(b).

186. *Steele,* see above note 5 at 1412.

187. *Wolski 2014,* see above note 3 at 94.

188. *Steele*, see above note 5 at 1387; *Sussman*, see above note 27 at 11.
189. *Wolski 2014*, see above note 3 at 99.
190. *Wolski 2014*, see above note 3 at 109; *Boulle,* see above note 7 at 65.
191. *Baril & Dickey,* see above note 56 at 4; *Pappas*, see above note 92 at 43.
192. SIAC–SIMC Arb–Med–Arb Protocol Art 8.
193. SIAC Rules do not expressly provide for party's termination of proceedings, but R 30.5 and Schedule 1.7 suggest that claims may be withdrawn. The Model Law (Arb) provides for termination by mutual consent (Art 32(2)(b)), and for claims to be withdrawn subject to objection from the respondent and at the discretion of the tribunal (Art 32(2)(a)).
194. SIAC Rules, R 11.1.
195. *Sussman*, see above note 27 at 12; *Steele*, see above note 5 at 1400.

Shall We Medi@?

By Phua Jun Han

I. Introduction

The use of online mediation, as part of online dispute resolution (ODR) in Singapore, is not completely new. It began in as early as 2001,[1] when a chatroom was launched to facilitate the resolution of neighbourly dispute. As it is still gaining momentum worldwide, various issues such as the governing law of the mediation settlement or the process as a whole will inevitably crop up. This paper will look at the more fundamental concerns of online mediation, and submit that while online mediation has its flaws, it ought not to be ruled out immediately. Online mediation is definitely not posited to completely replace traditional (i.e., face-to-face) mediation but it remains a strong option for parties' consideration, where the situation fits.

II. Concerns of online mediation

A. *Infrastructural support*

Earlier literature expressed the concern that the lack of access to computers[2] is itself a problem, since it strikes at the very foundation of online mediation. However, this problem, while present back in 1998, can be said to be of a relatively smaller concern in recent years, with a reported 82.7% household ownership of computers in Singapore as of 2013.[3] Going deeper than that, there is the concern that online mediation will favour parties that are more adept at IT skills,[4] or those that have an easier access to IT facilities.[5]

While no justification, one has to note that even traditional mediation is not free of biases. Traditional mediation tends to favour those with better physical and/or oratorical attributes,[6] or even social stature. As will be shown later, such subconscious impediments can be eroded by text-based online mediation. While this bias towards the more IT-savvy users may be present, it is submitted that this is a shortcoming that can be negated. While a third party may assist an individual in improving his or her IT skills, it is unlikely that the same can be done with respect to one's looks or oratorical skills or even social standing, at an equally low cost. Furthermore, with increased IT literacy among the population in this day and age, it is possible to say that this problem is of a lesser concern, given that modern users do not need complex technical knowledge to engage in video- or text-based communication.

B. Face-to-face interaction

One of the earliest critics of text-based[7] online mediation pointed out that unlike traditional mediation, face-to-face interaction among parties is removed[8] and the focus of mediation on the listening and processing of oral information is highly unlikely to be capable of translation to the online setting, hence creating potential impediments to communication. An irony arises herein to the extent that disputants' purported inability to communicate could have necessitated mediation in the first place.[9] Furthermore, mediators might be unable to use their physical presence to comfort parties and create a suitable environment for mediation.[10] One key contention in this area is the role played by body language and/or other non-verbal cues in mediation.

(1) Effective communication of message

Critics assert that emotions may not be fully communicated in the absence of body language or the use of voice tones[11] in the context of text-based online mediation. However, it is possible in certain scenarios that emotions have to be left out of the picture, in order to focus parties on the key issues. Yet again, emotions do remain at the core of certain disputes and they may have to be fully ventilated before parties may finally resolve their differences. Some argue that expressions of feelings done orally in a face-to-face setting "have a richer and more meaningful context than written expressions of feelings".[12]

Arguably, such critics may have failed to account for cultural change and adaptation.[13] As text-based communication such as WhatsApp and other instant messaging services infiltrate our lives, people have arguably adapted to communicating their messages through text-based mediums. The prevalence of text-based communication has increased our ability to convey messages through text that were previously seen as being capable of only being perceived physically.[14] The manipulation of emoticons and abbreviations in text messages also assist in communicating messages for all intents and purposes. For example "idk[15] :s" connotes a different meaning compared to "idk ☺", in that the former shows hesitancy by the communicator while the latter expresses a more easy-going malleability. Hence, the purported loss of expression and interplay needed for individuals to connect with and understand each other is provided for by the "dynamic"[16] nature of modern text-based communication. In fact, studies have shown that parties may feel that text-based communication allows parties more ease and confidence in expressing themselves, and, at the same time, decreases hostility between themselves with honest and open communication.[17]

(2) Role of body language

Amongst doubts surrounding the viability of online mediation, the lack of body language or non-verbal cues as illustrated above is the clearest.[18] The underlying assumption of such a concern seems to be that individuals can interpret accurately a communicant's thoughts through body language or non-verbal cues and the deprivation of this ability is hence a setback for mediation. This author challenges such an assumption to the extent that body language is open to misinterpretation[19] and may even be counter-productive. When a party perceives negative body language, whether there is a misinterpretation or not, he/she may tend to focus on and react to such perceived negative content, thus increasing the possibility of impasse due to possible retaliatory behaviour.[20] Not to undermine but to qualify this point, the reverse may definitely work as well, where a perception of a positive behaviour based on a possible misinterpretation may facilitate mediation as well. However, there seems to be a stronger likelihood that "warring parties" will tend to focus on the negative rather than the positive perceptions.

With a reliance on text-based communication, the distraction caused by non-verbal cues may arguably be eliminated and parties are better posited to focus their attention on the substantive issues rather than on the perceived negative emotional content by the other party.[21] Thus, such a forum actually assists parties in shifting away from a more confrontational to a comparatively constructive setting for dispute resolution. This could be especially useful in settings where emotions are highly charged and where parties have a history of constant exchange of negative verbal or non-verbal behavioural patterns, such as in acrimonious family situations.[22]

It definitely remains open for opponents to assert that text-based communication may actually cause an even greater unnecessary escalation of emotions, since there may be a tendency for individuals to not keep their emotions in check when engaging in e-communication. This could arguably be evident in the Singapore Government's campaigning of a "Safer Internet Day".[23] However, this concern could be set aside on the basis that the perceived "venom" in the Internet is set in a different context, since parties engaging in online mediation enter with a mindset of being engaged in non-litigious dispute resolution especially since they did so voluntarily.

Much of the discussion thus far has been on text-based mediation. However, online mediation includes the use of video-conferencing as well. While body language may not play a part in text-based online mediation, they may affect parties in communicating through video. The angles[24] from which mediators look into the camera may have a psychological impact as well, since parties may be subconsciously affected when a mediator or the other party does not appear to be gazing directly into the webcam.

(3) How physical presence affects trust

A key aspect of mediation is that of the mediator gaining the trust of parties during the process. Due to inherent biases that may surface in a physical setting, where a certain party may be more dominant, some mediators may lose control of the process. Even if they do not, it remains open for the other party to sense bias on the part of the mediator, or even feel slighted,[25] which may lead to even more hostility. This primarily arises in situations where a party feels that the other is allowed more "airtime" during joint sessions, or feel that the other party was given a longer private caucus. Text-based online mediation removes this barrier to the extent that parties are allowed the freedom to convey all the thoughts they have on their minds.

By allowing parties to fully ventilate their concerns, it may hence allow stronger faith in the system. Private caucuses may also be held simultaneously, which is impossible. Simultaneous text-based private caucuses not only bring up efficiency, but also remove the possibility of parties sensing bias due to the other party getting a purportedly longer private session, since there is no way of finding out in the first place.

(4) Impact of online mediation on fostering communication between parties

However, the effective substitution of the process of listening may compromise parties' ability to foster communication between each other,[26] since traditional mediation forces parties to listen to each other. The concern of "venomous messages" reflected earlier also casts even more doubts on such a process. However, synchronous communication, as afforded in traditional mediation, may also easily escalate a conflict, since a person's first response might not be the most reasonable or best.

On the other hand, asynchronous textual communication may actually afford parties the "cooling distance"[27] to process their emotional concerns before crafting a more appropriate response, hence making communication more focused and arguably lessening the likelihood of inflammatory language. This "cooling distance" is also assisted by the luxury of lag time afforded by text communication. Synchronous responses may not be as desirable due to the instant pressure they place on the recipient to respond. The lag time provided by text communication hence helps parties lighten the pressure they face, and thus calibrate their responses accordingly. Moreover, parties may have a further incentive to keep their language in check, given that text-based communication may be archived effort-lessly[28] and possibly be admissible evidence in criminal proceedings.

(5) Empowerment of parties

Online mediation also furthers the goals of mediation, to the extent that they include the fostering of empowerment[29] of parties as well. In cases involving family violence, the coerced party may not be at liberty to speak freely. Such a party may be wired to devoting his/her effort to pleasing the aggressor and any non-verbal cues that could be understood only between them may actually prevent the "victim" from speaking up. This is usually due to long-term isolation of the "victim" by the aggressor to the extent that the former develops a "total and exclusive dependence"[30] on the latter. By removing physical presence and non-verbal cues from the process, the "victim" may be more at liberty to speak up and communicate his/her concerns across more effectively. Hence, even if the dispute does not get resolved in the end, the party retains the opportunity to ventilate his/her concerns, which may not practically be available in the traditional mediation setting.

While the above analysis focuses primarily on cases of family violence, such ideas may be transplanted to other cases as well, where there is an imbalance of power between parties. An imbalance may arise from a difference in social stature, or even physical attributes such as appearance or oratorical delivery. The presence and need for neutrality of the mediator in a traditional setting may serve to perpetuate such an imbalance to the extent that parties may get "cowered" in a physical setting. While not purporting to correct this imbalance wholly, online mediation may serve to close up the gap, since parties may be more psychologically inclined to speak up, given the protective "shield" of the computer.

(6) The element of distance

Closely interlinked with the above is the element of physical distance between parties. One of the key concerns would be the lack of perception and interaction of body language among parties, as shown above. As mentioned earlier on the point of empowerment, the physical divide between parties may allow a meeker party to speak up more. A concern is that physical presence may arguably be needed to allow the mediator to use his or her physical presence to "set the parties at ease" and create a setting suitable for sustainable problem-solving.[31] Furthermore, it could be said that when parties are not "locked down" physically in a room, there might be a loss of momentum in resolving their disputes due to an "over-comfort" *vis-à-vis* their surroundings and a relative freedom from the element of time control. When parties are afforded more time to reflect, it might actually entrench them more deeply in their positions. However, it remains equally possible that parties may take the time and comfort afforded to reconsider and evaluate each other's interests. The answer hence seems to lie in the context of the dispute. Arguably, where emotions may be highly charged, such as in cases of family violence and where personal relationships are at stake, parties might be more willing to take a more reconciliatory approach when reflecting.

Physical proximity in traditional mediation may allow for mediators to intervene and cut out irrelevant issues. This ability could be lost when parties are allowed to type whatever they desire and flood the forum with inflammatory content. This could be solved by technical means, should service providers allow the mediator an emergency button to halt all communication and calm parties down. However, as stated earlier, parties may also be given the chance to process their thoughts before sending the message out, as compared to a spoken message, and this scenario may hence be rare.

Settlement agreements are also usually drafted and signed on the spot, so that parties may, in other words, "strike while the iron is hot". Arguably, such an advantage may be lost when mediation moves into the online sphere. However, text-based online mediation could make up for this disadvantage as it allows for a certain degree of permanence. Parties will have a more reliable source of agreed terms, as compared to contemporaneous notes, which are merely a reflection of perceived communication. Thus, parties will be better posited to draft the relevant settlement agreements with lesser effort. This advantage of permanence also extends to the process of mediation as well, since parties will now have the opportunity to refer to the mediator's opening statement[32] to remind themselves of their roles in the process, hence keeping parties more focused. In fact, studies have also shown that mediators agree that online text-based communication allows them to focus on the bigger picture instead of any specific interaction at any given moment.[33] Hence, online mediation not only forces the parties to focus on the key issues, but also facilitates the mediator's capability to do likewise.

Furthermore, the absence of physical proximity may allow for the calling of private caucuses more easily. Mediators no longer have to worry about parties' reactions or apprehensions about a perceived uneven devotion of time to the other party, as mentioned earlier. In a traditional mediation, proceedings may be disrupted in a rather unnatural manner in the calling of private caucuses. Even in video-based online mediation where the peculiarities of physical presence may surface yet again, the mediator may set up separate virtual rooms to caucus with the participants in private without causing much disturbance to the other party. Furthermore, the virtual setting allows for mediators to tap on a wealthy pool of professional knowledge as he can involve the participation of experts from afar,[34] subject to parties' consent. This could be the consultation of a psychologist, or someone well-versed in some commercial technical expertise. In a traditional setting, even if the physical presence of such experts do not cause parties any discomfort, it may cause parties to lose confidence in the mediator, questioning his expertise. Thus, not only does it reduce the discomforts of expert consultation, the process of doing so is eased greatly, since logistical concerns are greatly reduced.

In the long run, this access to third party support may allow for the training of younger mediators who may not have as much technical or subject-matter expertise. Hence, not only will it ease the process of mediation, online mediation may assist in the development of mediation generally as a field.

C. Confidentiality

While the permanence of text-based communication may be advantageous as shown earlier, it may also compromise the confidentiality of the process. One of the advantages that mediation has over litigation is that of confidentiality. However, the permanence of text-based communication makes it easier for parties to breach confidentiality since the archiving of communication is rather easy. Contents of a traditional mediation that are divulged may be challenged on grounds of contemporaneous notes but that might not work for instant text-based communication. Even if an injunction is granted against the dissemination of such contents, it might not be speedy enough to stop the initiation of the harm, which is made more easily.

This concern applies equally to video-conferencing mediation, where it is easier for parties to record proceedings, rather than sneaking in a voice recorder in a traditional mediation. Thus, while virtual mediation may assist parties, its very nature may also compromise the very fundamental which gains parties' trust and reliance, that being the element of confidentiality.

III. Moving forward

As global technological advancement forges ahead, coupled with increasing reliance on electronic communication, and based on which businesses may be transacted without reliance on other mediums, one may say that ODR is inevitable, and so is the option of online mediation. This is primarily due to the fact, which some elders may frown on, that we may be getting more comfortable with electronic rather than face-to-face communication. The alternative dispute resolution (ADR) movement ought to move along with the times and a key element is the reliance on improved communication. To resolve disputes more appropriately and preferably amicably, parties ought not to be forced into a mode of communication that they might be less comfortable with, since the traditional assumption that face-to-face communication is the most optimal medium of communication could ostensibly be challenged.

Despite the misgivings about online mediation, one has to note that sometimes without online mediation, there might not even be mediation in the first place, where parties get to communicate and voice their concerns.[35] Though this concern was raised in places such as the US where distance may play a key role, it is submitted that this point applies equally in the tiny "red dot" of Singapore as well. Even if parties may not be overseas, their schedules might not meet. One of the advantages that ADR has over litigation is that of speedy dispute resolution and ODR provides an even greater advantage than traditional ADR, by offering more flexibility in the arranging for a session. Even if parties may be willing to meet, a virtual setting might be more conducive for the generation of the

21st century even for community disputes, given the greater comfort with e-communication.

At the end of the day, while it is here to stay, online mediation ought not to exclude other forum options as well. There remain scenarios where traditional mediation may be a better option. Hence, it ought not to be seen as a battle between online mediation versus other methods of dispute resolution, such as traditional mediation. Instead, online mediation ought to be seen as a complementary tool in plugging in gaps and pioneering new frontiers in the ADR movement.

Endnotes

1. However, this chatroom is now defunct. Ngoh-Tiong Tan, "Community mediation in Singapore: Principles for community conflict resolution" (2002) 19 (3) *Conflict Resolution Quarterly* 289.
2. Joel B. Eisen, "Are We Ready for Mediation in Cyberspace?" (1998) *Brigham Young University Law Review* 1305 ("*Eisen*") at 1340.
3. "Infographics: Highlights of Household Expenditure Survey 2012/13", *Singstat* (2013) <http://www.singstat.gov.sg/docs/default-source/default-document-library/publications/publications_and_papers/household_income_and_expenditure/ssnsep14-pg7-14.pdf> (accessed on 15 October 2015) at 9.
4. Andrea M. Braeutigam, "Fusses That Fit Online: Online Mediation in Non-Commercial Contexts" (2006) 5 *Appalachian Journal of Law* 275 ("*Braeutigam*") at 291.
5. *Braeutigam*, see above note 4 at 291.
6. *Braeutigam*, see above note 4 at 291.
7. This could come in the form of chatrooms or email exchanges.
8. *Eisen,* see above note 2 at 1308.
9. *Eisen,* see above note 2 at 1309.
10. Ettore Maria Lombardi, "Is Online Mediation the Way to Fit the Forum to the Fuss?" (2012) 19 *Maastricht Journal of European and Comparative Law* 524 ("*Lombardi*") at 541.
11. *Lombardi*, see above note 10 at 539.
12. *Eisen*, see above note 2 at 1310.
13. *Braeutigam*, see above note 4 at 290.
14. This includes the use of emoticons and abbreviations such as "LOL", "wth", "ikr" … .
15. Abbreviation for "I don't know".

16. *Braeutigam*, see above note 4 at 290.
17. *Braeutigam*, see above note 4 at 290.
18. *Eisen*, see above note 2 at 1322.
19. *Braeutigam*, see above note 4 at 291.
20. *Braeutigam*, see above note 4 at 291.
21. *Braeutigam*, see above note 4 at 291.
22. *Braeutigam*, see above note 4 at 292.
23. Singapore Safer Internet Day website <http://www.saferinternetday.org/web/singapore/home> (accessed 15 October 2015).
24. Noam Ebner & Jeff Thompson, "@ Face Value? Nonverbal Communication & Trust Development in Online Video-Based Mediation" (2014) 2 *International Journal of Online Dispute Resolution* 1 at 29.
25. Llewellyn Joseph Gibbons, Robin M. Kennedy & Jon Michael Gibbs, "Cyber-Mediation: Computer-Mediated Communications Medium Massaging the Message" (2002) 32 *New Mexico Law Review* 27 ("*Gibbons, Kennedy & Gibbs*") at 54.
26. *Eisen*, see above note 2 at 1325.
27. *Braeutigam*, see above note 4 at 295.
28. Dafna Lavi, "Till Death Do Us Part?! — Online Mediation as an Answer to Divorce Cases Involving Violence" (2014–2015) 16 *North Carolina Journal of Law and Technology* 253 ("*Lavi*") at 286.
29. *Lavi*, see above note 28 at 294.
30. *Lavi*, see above note 28 at 267.
31. *Lombardi*, see above note 10 at 541.
32. *Gibbons, Kennedy & Gibbs*, see above note 24 at 59.
33. *Lavi*, see above note 28 at 302.
34. *Lavi*, see above note 28 at 284.
35. *Lavi*, see above note 28 at 299.

Good Faith Participation in Mediation

By Chan Min Hui

I. Introduction

This paper seeks to explore if a statutory **requirement of good faith participation during mediation** ("good faith participation requirement") should be imposed on the parties.[1] There has been extensive debate on this subject, particularly amongst US academics. This paper sets out to consider the debate in Singapore's context.

First, what *is* good faith participation during mediation? The nebulous concept of good faith may itself be a reason why a requirement of good faith participation will be discouraged. However, to gather a preliminary idea of what good faith participation is, one could think in terms of behaviour designed to achieve the objectives of mediation, i.e., to allow open communication about the parties' interests and relationship, and, possibly, the resolution of the dispute in a mutually beneficial manner.[2]

This paper posits that Singapore should not introduce a good faith participation requirement. While such a requirement can provide a safeguard against abuses of the mediation process and spur greater efficiency, there is no need for the requirement today. Mediations in Singapore are properly utilised in an efficient manner. Further, such a requirement can interfere with the voluntariness of the parties and compromise the confidentiality of the mediation process. This undermines the core values of mediation and diminishes the efficacy of mediation in helping parties find a sustainable solution in an amicable manner.

Following this, Part II will provide an introduction to mediations in Singapore. Parts III and IV will consider the strongest arguments, both for and against a statutory requirement of good faith participation in mediation, in Singapore's context. Part V will then evaluate the arguments and conclude that a statutory requirement of good faith participation need not and should not be introduced.

II. Mediation in Singapore

Courts have **strongly** encouraged the use of mediation to resolve disputes, although they have stopped short of making it mandatory.[3] The move away from litigation was not to reduce the courts' workload, but to resolve disputes in a non-confrontational way, so that the relationships between parties are preserved.[4] This reflects Singapore's desire for "softer" and more relational dispute resolution mechanisms.[5]

The courts' initiatives are manifested in developments such as the introduction of Order 59 Rule 5(c) (*r5(c)*) of the Rules of Court,[6] which allows the court to consider the "parties' conduct in relation to any attempt at resolving the matter … by mediation…". *r5(c)* has not been tested yet.[7] However, it is apparent that the broadness of the provision permits more than one understanding. The prevailing opinion is that *r5(c)* means that cost sanctions can be imposed on parties who do not reasonably consider the use of mediation, taking into account the parties' behaviour *before* mediation.[8] Alternatively, *r5(c)* can be interpreted to allow courts to consider the parties' behaviour during mediation.[9] This broad(er) interpretation is consistent with international practice — France,[10] Australia[11] and the UK[12] allow courts to take into account the parties' behaviour during mediation when apportioning costs.[13] However, for the sake of argument and clarity, this paper will limit the scope of *r5(c)* to allowing courts to consider whether a party has reasonably considered mediation, taking in account the parties' behaviour *before* the mediation session.[14]

III. Arguments for a good faith participation requirement

Proponents of a good faith participation requirement generally put forward these arguments:[15]

A. *Mediation requires good faith participation*

Mediation will not be viable if bad faith conduct is left unchecked.[16] This is because mediation is premised on open discussions between parties, bolstered by the facilitative effort of the mediator, to find a suitable resolution for the dispute.[17] With no formal discovery provisions or sanctions to encourage parties to share information in mediation, a good faith requirement seems pertinent in ensuring that the mediation process is not frustrated by parties' unwillingness to participate in the mediation in a manner aligned with the premise of mediation.[18]

This is particularly since lawyers often accompany their clients to mediation.[19] Lawyers (indeed, Singaporean lawyers are no exception![20]) are trained to be and accustomed to being adversarial.[21]

An example of how the mediation process could be abused in the absence of a good faith requirement is requesting mediation purely to fish for information that can subsequently be used as leverage.[22] Another example is requesting mediation purely to evaluate the potential effectiveness of the other party at trial.[23] Further, "Rambo-style"[24] litigators could simply request mediation to wear down a less financially endowed party,[25] by protracting the proceedings. The introduction of *r5(c)* could also incentivise parties to request for mediations purely to escape potential costs sanctions. An unwilling party to mediation, "compelled" by *r5(c)*, is more likely to engage in such process abuses, since there is no desire to resolve the dispute by mediation anyway.

Further, the benefits of mediation, e.g., the finding of appropriate solutions, or the improvement of relationships, will be thwarted if a party exhibits bad faith behaviour, such as engaging in "surface bargaining" (i.e., bargaining with no intent to resolve the dispute or consider the opinions of the other party). Users of mediation in Singapore value such benefits. Thus, a good faith participation requirement is imperative to safeguard the utility and value of the mediation process.

Lastly, is should be noted that a good faith participation requirement cannot prevent parties from obtaining additional information from parties or prevent the inevitable subconscious evaluation of the other side's effectiveness at trial. The argument here is that a good faith participation requirement would ensure that the mediation session is not wasted (by parties who *purely* engage in bad faith behaviour), since it compels parties to put in genuine efforts into the negotiations.

B. Ensuring time and cost efficiency

A good faith participation requirement would lead to greater time and cost efficiency. This is because parties who appear with the requested documents, appropriate settlement authority and a proper negotiating mind-frame[26] are likely to be able to engage in the mediation in a more productive way.[27] The desirability of cost and time efficiency is evident in Singapore, since users of mediation regard time and costs savings as important factors in determining whether they were satisfied with the outcome of mediation.[28]

IV. Arguments against a requirement of good faith participation in Singapore[29]

Of course, parties *should* participate in good faith during mediations.[30] However, some argue that there should not be a *statutory requirement* of good faith participation. This is due to the following reasons:

A. There is no need for a good faith participation requirement

Empirical evidence suggests that there is no need for a good faith participation requirement in Singapore today.[31] A recent survey revealed that:[32]

81% of the parties agreed that mediation helped to improve their relationship with the other party;

99% of the lawyers and parties would recommend mediation to others.[33]

Further, 87% of court-annexed mediations, and 75% of mediations under SMC settled.[34]

The high settlement rates, high satisfaction rates for the outcome of mediation and tendency of mediation to improve parties' relations cumulatively suggest that there is currently no problem of bad faith participation compromising on the values of mediation. Further, mediation sessions today are time- and cost-efficient, since many cases are settled within one day.[35]

B. *Mediator impartiality*

Mediator impartiality[36] is the bedrock of the mediation process in Singapore.[37] Since mediator impartiality is determined by the *parties'* own perceptions,[38] the perception of mediator partiality strongly disincentivises active participation in mediation by the parties.[39]

Assuming that the mediator would give evidence relating to whether a good faith participation requirement has been breached, it is argued that a good faith participation requirement compromises on mediator impartiality. This is because the duty to pass judgment on whether a party has participated in good faith is antithetical to the notion of mediator impartiality, which is built around the notion that the mediator should not express a normative or analytical critique.[40] One can see definitely the force in this argument: a mediator who is obliged to, and does, report the lack of good faith by a party (particularly if the court later dismisses this allegation) could be seen as lacking in impartiality.[41]

However, the conception of mediator impartiality in Singapore is different. There is a distinct faith in the expertise and impartiality of the mediator in Singapore.[42] This is evinced by the fact that parties do not view the mediator's evaluation of the merits of their case, or the mediator's suggestions as to settlement options or particular solutions during the mediation poorly. In fact, they appear to view such mediator interventions desirably.[43] Thus, unlike the model referred to above, neutrality is not built around the mediator's conscious forbearance from passing judgment.[44]

In Singapore, obliging the mediator to pass judgement on the presence of good faith behaviour might *enhance*, rather than compromise, the perception of mediator impartiality. This is due to a combination of the value of conforming to socially acceptable behaviour found in collectivist communities like Singapore,[45] as well as the faith in mediators. Thus, "calling out" the "misbehaving" party would likely comport with the Singaporean notion of "impartiality", tempered by social expectations of acceptable behaviour, more than condoning such behaviour.[46] Not doing so could instead result in the mediator being viewed as "protecting" the misbehaving party.[47]

C. Confidentiality[48]

The confidential nature of mediations underpins the utility and value of the mediation process.[49] Users of mediation in Singapore prize a conducive environment which allows them to express their views on the dispute.[50] The confidential nature of mediations invariably contributes to that environment by allowing for a private forum for the parties to discuss the dispute candidly,[51] without fear that commercially sensitive information would be revealed to the public.[52]

In Singapore, confidentiality is particularly important, since mediators are often expected to lead the mediation.[53] Parties are unlikely to participate actively in the mediation, if they are unable to trust the mediator,[54] such trust stemming from what is perceived as an important (and basic) role of the mediator — to keep information shared confidential.[55] This need for trust stemming from the mediator's promise to keep information confidential can be likened to the parties' trust in their psychiatrist.[56]

If there is a good faith participation requirement, courts would need evidence to decide if it has been breached.[57] Whether a statutory requirement of good faith should be introduced thus depends on the extent to which exceptions to confidentiality have to be introduced or extended to accommodate such a good faith requirement. In Singapore, the legal status of confidentiality of information relating to mediations is unclear,[58] not least because there is no unified statutory regime for confidentiality during mediations yet.[59] An exhaustive discussion of the principles relating to confidentiality[60] is beyond the scope of this paper; it suffices to say that *new* exceptions to confidentiality would be necessary to accommodate a good faith participation requirement.[61]

It can then be argued that a new, but *narrowly crafted* exception to confidentiality would tilt the balance in favour of a good faith participation requirement.[62] Two points should be highlighted in response.

First, the mere *prospect* of bad faith adjudication damages parties' faith in the confidentiality of mediation.[63] The fear of confidential information being divulged later strongly disincentivises active participation in mediations.[64] Since the utility of mediation is premised on the parties' active participation, the efficacy of mediation would be compromised as long as the spectre of bad faith adjudication exists.

Alternatively, narrowly crafted exceptions *can* alleviate the fear that confidentiality would be compromised. For example, such an exception could be in the form of a bare certification by the mediator[65] that a party has acted in bad faith.[66] However, such exceptions are undesirable, for it subtly creates increased pressure on the parties to go above and beyond to exhibit good faith behaviour to the mediator. This dangerously increases the potential that legitimate and productive behaviour is chilled, and entrenches on the parties' autonomy to present their case and decide in the matter they wish.

It should also be noted that a good faith participation requirement might sit uneasily with a contractual confidentiality clause binding parties not to disclose any information used in the mediation to third parties.[67] This is due to the competing considerations of party autonomy and the related notion of sanctity of contract on the one hand, and the public policy of not allowing the suppression of evidence on the other.[68]

Thus, the introduction of a requirement of good faith participation would require extremely compelling reasons.

D. Party self-determination

This refers to the value of allowing parties full decision-making power during mediation. Mediation in Singapore is developed on the premise of voluntariness,[69] since it is the promise of voluntariness which allows parties to have ownership of the mediation process and any consequent resolution (if applicable), leading to sustainable and appropriate resolutions.[70] Thus, it is not surprising that users of mediation in Singapore prize its voluntary nature.[71]

A requirement of good faith participation chills legitimate conduct, particularly if the requirement is phrased in a broad manner.[72] The fear of confidential information being revealed during adjudication on the alleged breach of the good faith participation requirement and sanctions for such breaches,[73] coupled with uncertainty as to what good faith participation means, is likely to modify the manner parties present their cases,[74] or make decisions.

This is problematic. First, parties might consequently feel that they do not have a fair proceeding.[75] Second, this may chill legitimate conduct and lead to counter-productive behaviour instead. For example, parties could perceive innocent mediator questions, such as those to reality-test the parties, as a subtle invitation for them to re-consider their decisions. Alternatively, parties *might* be pressurised into accepting a proposed solution that they are not entirely comfortable with, due to a (false) perception that not accepting what might be an "objectively reasonable" solution could be sanctionable conduct.[76] This can deter a party from fully discussing and evaluating its real interests during mediation, undermining the efficacy of mediation in promoting such discussions and in consequently resulting in sustainable and appropriate solutions.[77] Of course, the propensity of such scenarios happening may not be high — nevertheless, the potential of legitimate conduct being chilled should not be taken lightly, and compelling reasons are needed to justify a legislative decision to condone such a potential with the introduction of a good faith participation requirement.

E. Difficulty of defining the good faith requirement

It has been argued that existing legal authorities establishing good faith requirements elsewhere do not give clear guidance about what conduct is prohibited.[78] This chills legitimate mediation behaviour by the parties,[79] undermining mediation's efficacy.

In Singapore, these concerns might be alleviated with *HSBC's* emphatic holding that there is a "core concept" of good faith, which "encompasses the threshold subjective requirement of acting honestly, as well as the objective requirement of observing accepted commercial standards of fair dealing in the performance of the identified obligations. This encompasses a duty to act fairly, having regard to the legitimate interests of the other party."[80]

However, two problems should be highlighted.

First, this definition is meant to allow *courts* to determine whether there has been a breach of a good faith obligation — the chilling effect on parties' legitimate behaviour during mediations is unlikely to be alleviated by this definition, not least because parties would be unsure if their personal conceptions of "honesty" and "commercial standards of fair dealing" would comport with the courts' conception. This is particularly since mediation is a different dispute resolution process from litigation, where most judicial applications and definitions of "good faith" or "honesty" or "fairness" exist. Thus, there is a paucity of guidance as to what these values mean.

Further, *HSBC's* standard of "good faith" behaviour is onerous. Where mediation is needed, trust and discussion between parties would have usually broken down,[81] and misconceptions will usually abound. Thus, it is impractical to demand parties to first objectively decipher what the "legitimate interests of the other party" are, and, subsequently, to have regard to them. In addition, *HSBC* held that on its facts, the good faith obligation related to a common goal of the parties, and faithfulness to this "purpose" meant that parties cannot attempt to unfairly profit from the known ignorance of the other. In turn, this meant that the parties must disclose *all* material information which could impact the negotiations or the achievement of the purpose of the clause.[82]

Admittedly, the good faith obligation does not always require a full disclosure of material facts. However, the intrusive result of requiring full disclosure, even though the respondent's non-disclosure has not actually prejudiced the appellant[83] highlights the strictness of *HSBC's* "good faith" standard. This is problematic as it has the potential of pressurising the parties at mediation to settle, for fear of contravening a strict good faith standard. Further, parties might altogether be turned away from mediation if they perceive such "good faith" participation to be contrary to their commercial interests.

Of course, a good faith participation requirement does not have to adopt *HSBC's* core concept of "good faith"; it could be argued that it would be productive to have a good faith requirement that concretises prohibited behaviour into non-intrusive standards capable of ready ascertainment by parties. However, such an ideal good faith standard that embodies the arguments for a good faith participation requirement and circumvents the arguments against such a requirement is elusive.

Good faith participation standards can be broken down into procedural and substantive standards.[84] Procedural standards refer to requirements such as requiring the exchange of documents requested by the mediator or the mediation agency, or that parties state their positions, and be there (or have someone there) to hear the other parties' position.[85] While productive, legitimate conduct would not be consequently discouraged by such procedural standards, the utility of such is limited. Mere compliance with procedure does little to prevent bad faith conduct, such as surface bargaining, or participating in mediation purely for extraneous reasons. Thus, such procedural requirements are not really "good faith" standards that safeguard the utility and integrity of the mediation process; they are merely procedural requirements relating to mediation. The introduction of such procedural requirements can be helpful, although the potential of confidentiality being compromised must be noted when crafting such procedural requirements and its attendant confidentiality exception.

On the other hand, substantive good faith participation requirements refer to requirements that compel parties to participate in the mediation process in a substantive manner. An example is a provision requiring for parties to participate in "meaningful discussions".[86] These are truly good faith standards that safeguard the value of mediations and the integrity of the mediation process, by compelling the parties to conform to the premises of mediation, e.g., joint problem-solving through open discussions. However, such requirements compromise on confidentiality and party autonomy, as elaborated on above. The inherent vagueness of such requirements, which inevitably warrants an investigation into subjective states of minds, coupled with the paucity of case illustrations, might also altogether turn parties away from commercial mediations.[87] This contradicts the vision of making Singapore a hub for dispute resolution.[88]

V. Conclusion

A substantive requirement of good faith participation should not be introduced.[89] Mediation is rarely abused in Singapore. Thus, the drawbacks of such a requirement, particularly the inevitable compromise on the confidential and voluntary nature of mediation and the consequent chilling of legitimate mediation behaviour, far outweigh its benefits.[90] *r5(c)* should likewise not be construed as allowing the courts to consider whether parties *participated* in mediation in good faith.[91]

In the future, if abuses of the mediation process become an increasing trend, more time would have to be devoted to addressing the drawbacks of introducing a requirement of good faith participation first. To this end, it is important for more empirical research to be done to gather the perceptions of the users of mediation, as mediation is ultimately a party-centric process, and its continued usage would have to depend on rules that comport with the users' understanding of the values of mediation and preferences for certain desirable traits of mediation.[92]

Endnotes

1. Whether a good faith participation obligation contractually agreed between the parties is enforceable or desirable is beyond the scope of this paper. However, on the enforceability of such obligations, see *International Research Corp PLC v Lufthansa Systems Asia Pacific* [2013] 1 *Singapore Law Reports* 973 at [90]–[97], upheld on appeal on this point: see *International Research Corp PLC v Lufthansa Systems Asia Pacific* [2014] 1 SLR 130 at [54] and *HSBC Institutional Trust Services (Singapore) Ltd v Toshin Development Singapore Pte Ltd* [2012] 4 *Singapore Law Reports* 738 ("*HSBC*"), particularly at [48] and [43]. It seems likely that a contractual provision to mediate in good faith would be enforceable. Thus, parties can consider inserting such a provision in their contract.

2. This is only a working idea intended to provide readers less acquainted with the idea of good faith participation in mediations with a semblance of what this means. It is in the hope that this would facilitate the reader's understanding of the paper.

3. Joyce Low & Dorcas Quek, "Introducing a Presumption of ADR for Civil Matters in the Subordinate Courts" *Singapore Law Gazette* (May 2012) <http://www.lawgazette.com.sg/2012-05/415.htm> (accessed 3 November 2015) ("*Introducing a Presumption of ADR*"); Danny McFadden & George Lim S.C., eds., *Mediation in Singapore: A Practical Guide* (Singapore: Sweet and Maxwell, 2015) ("*Mediation in Singapore*") at [13.036]; Sundaresh Menon C.J., "Response by Chief Justice Sundaresh Menon, Opening of Legal Year 2014" *Singapore Academy of Law* (3 January 2014) <http://www.sal.org.sg/Lists/Speeches/Attachments/119/OLY%202014%20CJ's%20Speech.pdf> (accessed 3 November 2015) at [30].

   There are exceptions in a few areas of law. For example, in family disputes, s. 50(3A) of the Women's Charter (Cap 353, 2009 Rev. Ed.) provides for mandatory mediation if there is a child below 8 years old involved. S. 15 of the Community Mediation Centres Act (Cap 49A, Rev. Ed.) allows magistrates to refer the complaint to the Community Mediation Centre with or without the consent of the parties. Mediation for cases filed in the Small Claims Tribunal are also mandatory: s. 17 of the Small Claims Tribunal Act (Cap. 308, 1998 Rev. Ed.).

Dorcas Quek in *Mediation in Singapore* (see above note 3) states that the process of "consultation" is actually mediation.

4. *Introducing a Presumption of ADR,* see above note 3; Joel Lee & Teh Hwee Hwee, eds., *An Asian Perspective on Mediation* (Singapore: Academy Publishing, 2009) (*"Asian Perspective"*) at [3.34]. C.f. other countries, where the use of dispute mechanisms other than litigation, such as mediation, is at least in part motivated by the need to reduce case backlog.

5. Andrew Phang JA, "Alternate Dispute Resolution and Regional Prosperity — A View From Singapore" (2014), Supreme Court of Singapore <https://www.supremecourt.gov.sg/data/doc/ManagePage/5522/China-ASEAN%20Justice%20Forum%20-%20ADR%20and%20Regional%20Prosperity%20(Final)%2011092014%20(Phang%20JA)%20highlighted.pdf> (accessed 3 November 2015) (*"Phang JA"*) at [16]; *Asian Perspective,* see above note 4 at [3.34]; Goh Joon Seng, "Mediation in Singapore: The Law and Practice", Asean Law Association (2003) <http://www.aseanlawassociation.org/docs/w4_sing2.pdf> (accessed 3 November 2015) (*"Goh Joon Seng"*) at 159.

6. Rules of Court (Cap 322, R 5, 2014 Rev Ed).

7. The closest a court has ever come to applying *r5(c)* or its underlying principles seem to be in *HSBC*, where parties were ordered to bear their own costs both at the appeal and at the proceedings below, subsequent to the observation that "the Parties' dispute is a matter that ought to have been resolved by the application of commercial common sense in good faith through the mediation process, rather than through the adversarial curial process". *HSBC*, see above note 1 at [68] and [72]. Note that *r5 (c)* was not mentioned in *HSBC*.

8. *Mediation in Singapore*, see above note 3 at [13.036], [9.046]; *Phang JA*, see above note 5 at [10].

9. Joel Lee, "Court-based Initiatives for Mediation in Singapore" (2011) *Asian JM* 60 (*"Court-based initiatives"*) at 18.

10. Nadja Alexander, *International and Comparative Mediation: Legal Perspectives* (The Netherlands: Wolters Kluwer, 2009) (*"International and Comparative Mediation"*) at 332.

11. In *Capolingua v Phylum* (1991) 5 WAR 137 , the Supreme Court of Western Australia refused to award costs to the successful defendant for several reasons, including its unreasonable conduct during mediation, which meant the trial was lengthened considerably. In Queensland, legislation also allows for the imposition of cost sanctions against parties who fail to attend mediation or who impede mediators during the process. *International and Comparative Mediation,* see above note 10 at 332.

12. For example, in the English case of *Earl of Malmesbury v Strutt and Parker* [2007] EWCH 999 (QBD), the court considered the application of cost sanctions in relation to a party's unreasonable behaviour in mediation. The plaintiff ultimately prevailed in court. However, the amount eventually awarded to the plaintiff was less than both what he claimed for, as well as his final offer made during the prior mediation session. This is because the court thought that the claimant did act unreasonably during the mediation, and took this into account when determining costs. Privilege was waived in respect of all "without prejudice" matters, so that evidence from the mediation could be considered when determining costs ([24]). In doing so, the court held that the claimants' offer of 9m plus 80% of the claimant's costs (compared to the defendant's offer of 1m inclusive of interest with each side to bear their own costs) was "plainly unrealistic and unreasonable" ([71]–[72]). In the UK, the Civil Procedure rules mean that courts may take into account the behaviour of the parties before and after the proceedings, including their attempts to solve the dispute. *International and Comparative Mediation*, see above note 10 at p 334.

13. Note that the provisions are different.

14. I consider the time limit imperative, as the lack of a time limit could easily result in *r5(c)* being used to consider whether a party has acted reasonably during the mediation session, since unreasonable participation during the mediation could be construed as a manifestation of the failure to consider the use of mediation reasonably.

15. See, for example, John Lande, "Using Dispute System Design Methods to Promote Good-Faith Participation in Court-Connected Mediation Programs" (2009] 50 *UCLA Law Review* 69 (*"John Lande"*) at 77; Roger L. Carter, "Oh, Ye of Little (Good Faith): Questions, Concerns and Commentary on Efforts to Regulate Participant Conduct in Mediations" (2002] *Journal of Dispute Resolution* 367 (*"Carter"*) at 373; Carol L. Izumi & Homer C. La Rue, "Prohibiting Good Faith Reports under the Uniform Mediation Act: Keeping the Adjudication Camel out of the Mediation Tent" (2003) *Journal Of Dispute Resolution* 67 (*"Izumi &Homer"*) at 77.

16. Kimberlee K. Kovach, "Good Faith in Mediation-Requested, Recommended, or Required? A New Ethic" (1997) 38 South Texas Law Review 575 (*"Kovach"*) at 590–595; E. Sherman, "Court Mandated Alternative Dispute Resolution: What Form of Participation is Required?" 46 *SMU Law Review* 2079 (*"E Sherman"*) at 2089. Note that the author is writing about alternative dispute resolution mechanisms in general, not specifically mediations.

17. *Mediation in Singapore,* see above note 3 at [15.048]; Lawrence Boulle & Teh Hwee Hwee, *Principles, Process, Practice* (Singapore: Butterworths Asia, 2000) (*"Principles, Process, Practice"*) at 8–9; State Court Code of Ethics at Art 4.1; Ruth Charlton & Micheline Dewdney, *The Mediator's Handbook* (Sydney: Lawbook Company, 2nd Edition, 2004) (*"Charlton and Dewdney"*) at 320; Kimberlee K. Kovach, "Lawyer Ethics in Mediation: Time for a Requirement of Good Faith in Mediation" (1997 Winter) 4 *Dispute Resolution Magazine* 9 (*"Kovach Mag"*) at 9; *Kovach,* see above note 16 at 595.

18. *Izumi and Homer,* see above note 15 at 70.

19. There are no published statistics in support of this point. However, anecdotal evidence supports this proposition. Further, the authors in *Principles, Process, Practice* note that "mediation is often chosen on the advice of lawyers, either before or after legal proceedings have been instituted. Parties in self-selected mediations also look to lawyers for assistance." *Principles, Process, Practice,* see above note 17 at 143–144.

20. *Court-based initiatives,* see above note 9 at [3]; *Mediation in Singapore,* see above note 3 at [8.007].

21. *Kovach,* see above note 16 at 593.

22. *Kovach,* see above note 16 at 593; Chiara-Marisa Caputo, "Lawyers' Participation in Mediation" (2007) 18 *Australasian Dispute Resolution Journal* 84 (*"Caputo"*) at 87–88.

23. *Kovach,* see above note 16 at 594. Generally, see *Kovach* at 593–595.

24. *Izumi and Homer,* see above note 15 at 70.

25. *Caputo,* see above note 22 at 87–88.

26. Assuming these are facets of the good faith requirement — they often are: see, for example, the good faith participation benchmarks proposed in *Kovach.*

27. *Izumi and Homer,* see above note 15 at 71–72.

28. *Principles, Process, Practice,* see above note 17 at 294.

29. There are other very forceful arguments put forth that have unfortunately not been considered, due to the constraints of this paper. For example, some critics have highlighted that a statutory good faith participation requirement would be antithetical to the lawyer's duty to his client. See, for example,

International and Comparative Mediation, above note 10 at 236–239; *Kovach,* see above note 16 at 604. Alternatively, it has also been argued that a good faith participation requirement could lead to unproductive satellite litigation, particularly due to the vagueness of the concept of "good faith". However, the introduction of *r5(c)* has not led to any such satellite litigation thus far, some 4.5 years after its introduction. Thus, this argument does not appear to be as relevant in Singapore.

30. Joel Lee, "Agreements to Negotiate in Good Faith" (2013) *Singapore Journal of Legal Studies* 212 ("*Joel Lee*") at 218; *Aiton Australia v Transfield* [1999] NSWCSC 996 at [124]; *Principles, Process, Practice,* see above note 17 at 143; *Kovach,* see above note 16 at 590.

31. *Izumi and Homer* also warns that even in the US, some argue that good faith requirements are overreactions to a numerically small number of incidents, and that for egregiously bad conduct in mediation, good faith requirements are unnecessary. *Izumi and Homer,* see above note 15 at 77.

32. This survey was administered by the State Courts' Primary Dispute Resolution Centre for mediations of claims within the Magistrate's Court jurisdiction, between 2013 and 2014.

    Thomson Reuters and the State Courts' Joint Media Release at "Joint Launch of the State Courts' Centre for Dispute Resolution and Mediation in Singapore: A Practice Guide a Thomson Reuters Publication" (4 March 2015) <https://www.statecourts.gov.sg/NewsAndEvents/Documents/Media%20Release%20Joint%20Launch%20of%20the%20State%20Courts%20Centre%20for%20Dispute%20Resolution%20and%20Mediation%20in%20Singapore.pdf> (accessed 3 November 2015) ("*Joint Media Release*").

    It is important to note that the survey findings are based on quite a small sample size. To this end, more on-the-ground research and empirical evidence would be helpful in developing the field of mediation, particularly as Singapore is still adapting the Western model for appropriate use in Singapore. Mediations under the Singapore Mediation Centre ("SMC") are also in line with such favourable statistics: over 2300 matters have been mediated at the SMC, with about 75% of the cases settling, 90% of those settled being settled in one working day, 84% of the parties agreeing that mediation resulted in cost savings and 88% agreeing that it resulted in time savings. A further 94% of the parties agreed that they would recommend the process to other parties in the same conflict situation. (Statistics are published on SMC's website; see SMC website <http://www.mediation.com.sg/about-us/#our-statistics> (accessed 3 November 2015) ("*SMC Statistics*").

33. *Joint Media Release,* see above note 32. This is corroborated by statistics provided by Loong Seng Onn, "Mediation", in *Articles on Singapore Law,* 2015 at 3.4.3: 94% of the parties would recommend mediation to other persons in the same situation. <http://www.singaporelaw.sg/sglaw/laws-of-singapore/overview/chapter-3> (accessed 3 November 2015).

34. *Mediation in Singapore,* see above note 3 at [1.013]: 87% of the 23, 096 mediations in the State Courts were settled in 2009, 88% of the 20,154 mediations were settled in 2010, and 87% of the 14, 948 were settled from January to September 2011. The 75% figure is an approximate one. *SMC Statistics*, see above note 32.

35. For mediations under the SMC, refer to *SMC Statistics*; see above note 32. For mediations under the State Courts, see the information sheet on Mediation, provided by the State Courts. Singapore State Courts, "Mediation" (undated) <https://www.statecourts.gov.sg/CivilCase/Documents/Mediation.pdf> (accessed 3 November 2015).

36. It has been noted that "mediator impartiality" is used interchangeably with "neutrality", and might not admit of clear meaning as such. Here, "mediator impartiality" refers to the mediator not favouring one part or one side more than the other. Christopher W. Moore, *The Mediation Process: Practical Strategies for Resolving Conflict* (San Francisco: Jossey-Bass, 3rd Edition, 2003) (*"Moore"*) at 291.

37. In SMC's survey of the satisfaction levels of mediation users in Singapore, a strong correlation was found between the impartiality of mediators, and the satisfaction of the parties in relation to the outcome of the mediation. *Principles, Process, Practice*, see above note 17 at 293; *Izumi and Homer*, see above note 15 at 83.

38. *Izumi and Homer*, see above note 15 at 84.

39. *Izumi and Homer*, see above note 15 at 84.

40. *Izumi and Homer*, see above note 15 at 83.

41. *Izumi and Homer*, see above note 15 at 73.

42. This could be a perpetuation of the respect for the mediator in traditional versions of mediation, derived from the parties' faith in his integrity, expertise and experience. *Asian Perspective,* see above note 4 at 1.16.

43. Survey results suggest that a mediator's evaluation of the merits of a case, or assistance in the evaluation of the case did not compromise on mediator impartiality (the limited sample size of this survey must be noted). *Principles, Process, Practice*, see above note 17 at 299.

44. Of course, the Singaporean perspective presumes that the mediator acts according to the ethical standards imposed, and does not abuse the mediation process.

45. *Asian Perspective*, see above note 4 at [3.36].

46. *Kovach* makes a similar point: she argues that the mediator has a professional duty to set parameters and be in control of the process. Making an assessment or determination of the good faith nature of the parties' participation would come within this role. *Kovach*, see above note 16 at 601.

47. In *Charlton and Dewdney* (see above note 17 at 200), it is also noted that a mediator who allows one party to flaunt the courtesy or non-interruption guidelines on an ongoing basis may be perceived as favouring that party or at least disadvantaging the other party.

48. It is acknowledged that a good faith participation requirement would go some way in ensuring that confidential information is not revealed by the other party, as this is arguably bad faith behaviour. However, as argued, it is unlikely that bad faith behaviour is at all common in Singapore now. Therefore, the problems with exceptions to confidentiality far outweigh the benefits brought by a good faith participation requirement, where confidentiality is concerned.

49. *Izumi and Homer,* see above note 15 at 84; Maureen A. Weston, "Checks on Participant Conduct in Compulsory ADR: Reconciling the Tension in the Need for Good-Faith Participation, Autonomy and Confidentiality" (2001] 76 *Indiana Law Journal* 591 ("*Weston*") at 633.

50. *Principles, Process, Practice*, see above note 17 at 293–294.

51. Whether in joint discussions or private sessions with the mediator.

52. Jo-Anne Bigham, "Confidentiality and Without Prejudice: Illusory or Real?" (2006) 1 *Asian JM* 13 ("*Confidentiality and Without Prejudice*") at 14–15; *Weston,* see above note 49 at 633; *Izumi and Homer,* see above note 15 at 84, 86; *Principles, Process, Practice*, see above note 17 at 42.

53. *Asian Perspective,* see above note 4 at [4.15]; [3.62].

54. *Principles, Process, Practice*, see above note 17 at 126.

55. *Confidentiality and Without Prejudice*, see above note 52 at 15; *Izumi and Homer*, see above note 15 at 84; *Principles, Process, Practice*, see above note 17 at 127.

56. *Confidentiality and Without Prejudice*, see above note 52 at 15.

57. *Kovach*, see above note 16 at 692; *Weston*, see above note 49 at 641.

58. *Goh Joon Seng*, see above note 5 at 161; *Principles, Process, Practice*, see above note 17 at 344.

59. The Working Group suggested that a section on confidentiality be introduced into the proposed Mediation Act. They recommended: provision should be made to clarify the position on confidentiality and privilege in the context of mediation and the circumstances under which communications made in the

course of a mediation session are protected. It is recommended that statutory provisions could be introduced to ensure the preservation of confidentiality between parties, between parties and third parties, and between parties and the Courts. Recommendations of the Working Group to Develop Singapore into a Centre for International Commercial Mediation (3 December 2013) <https://www.mlaw.gov.sg/content/dam/minlaw/corp/News/FINAL%20 ICMWG%20Press%20Release%20-%20Annex%20A.pdf> (accessed 3 November 2015).

60. Including principles relating to privilege.

61. There are currently three broad categories which provide for confidentiality of mediations. They are: the without prejudice privilege, the common law action for breach of confidence, as well as statutory protection of confidentiality in some scenarios (community disputes, disputes over children etc. — women's charter) — see PPP. The first two are unlikely to be construed as covering good faith behaviour. Note that a provision in the community mediations act is capable of being construed as an exception to confidentiality that is wide enough to include evidence which shows the parties' lack of good faith when participating in mediations.

62. *Kovach*, see above note 16 at 602–603; *Weston*, see above note 49 at 638–642.

63. *John Lande*, see above note 15 at 102; *Carter*, see above note 15 at 392.

64. *John Lande*, see above note 15 at 105.

65. Most articles assume that the mediators would be the ones reporting non-good faith behaviour. This is only logical. If parties were to report such behaviour instead, it would likely be a scenario where party A asserts that party B breached the good faith participation requirement, whereas party B refutes that he breached the requirement. This will be less helpful than if the mediator, who is perceived as a neutral, gives evidence. However, see *John Lande* (see above note 15 at p 103), where the author points out that the mediator's testimony itself may not be reliable, as the mediator might emphasise facts consistent with that conclusion and downplay inconsistent facts.

66. *Kovach*, see above note 16 at 602.

67. These are commonly found. For example, clause 3 of the SMC Mediation Agreement, which has to be agreed to by both parties for a mediation under the auspices of the Singapore Mediation Centre to occur, stipulates that all persons involved in the mediation is to keep all information relating to the mediation confidential. It also stipulates that parties agree not to call mediators as witness or expert in relation to any proceedings relating to the dispute.

68. *Confidentiality and Without Prejudice*, see above note 52 at 20.

69. Voluntariness is used interchangeably with party self-determination here.

70. E. Sherman states that "the commanding role of the parties in determining their own resolution of the dispute under ADR is an important factor in explaining why there is a greater compliance rate with judgments resulting from settlement than from court-imposed decrees"; *Izumi and Homer*, see above note 15 at 80.

71. A survey revealed that the lack of pressure to settle by the mediator was a common feature associated with parties' satisfaction in relation to the outcome of mediation and the mediation process. *Principles, Process, Practice*, see above note 17 at 293–294.

72. *John Lande*, see above note 15 at 86.

73. *Izumi and Homer*, see above note 15 at 82.

74. *E Sherman*, see above note 16 at 2094.

75. *E Sherman*, see above note 16 at 2094.

76. See E. Sherman, "Good Faith in Mediation: Aspirational, not Mandatory" (1997) 4 *Dispute Resolution Magazine* 14 ("*E Sherman Mag*") at 14. This perception could arise from trends that have emerged elsewhere: Carter states that in bad faith cases, courts inevitably give lip service to the principle that parties cannot be compelled to settle. However, the same courts hold that offering $500 or $1000 to settle a case is out of bad faith. *Carter*, see above note 15 at 395.

77. *Carter*, see above note 15 at 393–396.

78. *Izumi and Homer*, see above note 15 at 74.

79. *John Lande*, see above note 15 at 86.

80. Further, what constitutes "reasonable commercial standards of fair dealing" will depend heavily on the commercial nature and purpose of the contract in question (*HSBC*, see above note 1 at [49]). Even though this was laid down in a case dealing with whether an express contractual obligation to negotiate in good faith is enforceable, the court stated that "in principle, there is no difference between an agreement to negotiate in good faith and an agreement to submit the dispute in mediation" (*HSBC* at [43]). Thus, it must be a forceful argument that the "core concept" is to be applied in the context of a statutory obligation of good faith participation in mediation as well (*HSBC* at [45]. Note that *HSBC* is a Court of Appeal case.

81. *Mediation in Singapore,* see above note 3 at [15.048].

82. *HSBC*, see above note 1 at [51], including information a commercial party obtained for its own commercial use.

83. *HSBC*, see above note 1 at [57].
84. Most commentators appear to draw the distinction between objective and subjective good faith standards, with objective standards referring to standards the breach of which can be objectively determinable. In practice, such standards typically refer to procedural rules and orders, or the exchange of forms. Subjective standards would be more closely linked to parties' intent. However, like Carter, I prefer the procedural/substantive dichotomy, as I believe that the use of the labels "objective" and "subjective" effectively concerns the substantive/procedural dichotomy. *Carter*, see above note 15 at 379.
85. Adapted from *E Sherman,* see above note 16 at 2097. Note that when Sherman talks about **minimal meaningful participation**, he suggests that there are different standards for such participation depending on which ADR is used. Having a party state his position and listen to the other parties' position was suggested specifically for mediation.
86. This is 001(f) of Kovach's proposed Code. *Kovach*, see above note 16 at 622.
87. In spite of cost sanctions, which are likely to be disproportionately low, compared to the value placed on confidentiality and certainty in commercial mediations.
88. K. Shanmugam, Minister of Law, quoted in a newspaper article. "New Singapore International Mediation Centre Launched", *Today* (5 Nov 2014) <http://www.todayonline.com/new-singapore-international-mediation-centre-launched> (accessed 3 November 2015).
89. In coming to this conclusion, I note that other legislatures have imposed a good faith participation requirement. See, for example, s11 of the Farm Debt Mediation Act 1994 (NSW) and s31(1)(b) of the Native Title Act 1993 (Cth) in Australia.
90. *Izumi and Homer* put it forcefully and succinctly: in sum, subtle forms of coercion through vigorous judicial enforcement of a requirement to mediate in good faith threaten to erode the integrity of the mediation process. *Izumi and Homer*, see above note 15 at 98.
91. C.f. *Joel Lee*, see above note 30.
92. There are currently no surveys gathering the perceptions of a good faith requirement, however crafted, from users of mediation. Further to the suggestion above, an example of gathering empirical evidence could be to use samples of such requirements to assess the appropriate meaning to attribute to "good faith", the breadth of the good faith requirement as well as the breadth of the accompanying confidentiality exceptions.

Bridging the Concepts of Neutrality and Power Imbalance

By Tan Ting Wei Kelly

I. Introduction

The neutrality of the mediator has often been referred to as one of the central philosophical concepts of mediation.[1] It is a term that is very much inseparable from the entire mediation process. However, there are doubts as to whether the neutrality of the mediator conflicts with the other powers that a mediator possesses, specifically the ability to address power imbalances. At first blush, these two concepts seem to be paradoxical and at odds with each other. However, the potential inequality that would arise from power imbalances mandates that the mediator should intervene to balance the power. This paper seeks to discuss whether mediator neutrality and the ability to address power imbalances are mutually exclusive concepts, and to explore if there is any possibility for both concepts to co-exist in the same spectrum. The first part of this paper will discuss the dichotomy between neutrality and the ability to address power imbalance. The paper will then move on to show that both concepts can in fact be reconciled with each other. Lastly, the paper will then critique the role of neutrality in mediation today.

II. The dichotomy between neutrality and power imbalance

A. *The notion of neutrality and impartiality*

Neutrality is a multi-dimensional concept with many different meanings attached to it. Broadly speaking, neutrality encompasses the following factors: that the mediator has no direct interest in the outcome of the dispute, has no prior knowledge of the dispute, is not associated with the parties, will not pass judgment of any sort and that the mediator will act even-handedly, fairly and without bias to the parties.[2] Neutrality and impartiality have been used inter-changeably[3] and are treated as synonymous with each other.[4] This approach is also one that is adopted by the State Courts of Singapore. In the *Code of Ethics and Basic Principles on Court Mediation*, the core principles of how mediation should be conducted defines impartiality as remaining neutral in all mediation proceedings. This reflects how impartiality is being equated to neutrality. Similarly, in the Singapore Mediation Centre Code of Conduct, the definition of impartiality also incorporates the notion of neutrality.

It is possible to distinguish between neutrality and impartiality by saying that neutrality refers to disinterestedness, while impartiality refers to fairness.[5] However, in practice, neutrality and impartiality often shade into each other and are divided by a paper-thin line. It is the author's view that neutrality and impartiality are coterminous. However, the aim of this paper is not to delve into the semantic differences, if any, between the two terms. Instead, this paper will treat neutrality and impartiality as the same, for the purposes of analysing the interplay between neutrality and power imbalances.

B. *Neutrality vs power imbalance*

Just like how neutrality is a central defining feature of mediation,[6] power imbalances are also a fixture in mediation proceedings. Every time a mediator sits down to help two parties resolve a dispute, the issue of a potential power imbalance emerges.[7] Imbalances can be identified in terms of gender; culture; generation; one-shot and repeat players; the individual and the big institution; the legally and non-legally aided; the inarticulate and the assertive; the wealthy and the not so wealthy; the knowledgeable and the ignorant or ill-advised.[8] Mediators possess the innate ability to address power imbalances.[9] This ability arises from the mediator's control over the entire mediation process. Moore has listed 12 forms of influence which a mediator can use to address power imbalances.[10] This would include managing the individual agenda items and controlling the order in which they are discussed, helping parties identify what information has to be exchanged, modifying the physical setting of the negotiation, as well as governing the timings in negotiation. Such intervention can range from being highly directive to being minimally interventionist. However, it is important to note that even at a minimalist level, the mediation process itself does indirectly moderate some power differences between the parties.[11]

It has been acknowledged that mediators have the power to address imbalances. The problem is that when a mediator chooses to balance the power, a conflict arises in relation to the mediator's neutrality. This is because if mediators are to redress an imbalance of power, they must do more than treat the parties equally. They must compensate for that imbalance by treating the parties unequally.[12] For example, a mediator could allocate more time for the weaker party to speak, instead of treating both parties equally by allocating the same amount of time to both of them. Such acts of the mediator go against the meaning of neutrality, which states that the mediator is to treat parties fairly and without bias. Thus, dealing with power while maintaining neutrality places mediators in a double bind.[13] Some academics have argued that the only way that a claim that mediators can address imbalances of power can stand up, is if mediators openly forego the neutrality rhetoric, and make their intervention on behalf of the party who is at a power disadvantage transparent.[14] This therefore places an ultimatum on mediators to either relinquish their neutrality by intervening, or retain their neutrality by not intervening.[15]

However, the danger of leaving power imbalances unaddressed is that it carries with it the possibility of the strongest disputant imposing a settlement that seems grossly unfair, when measured against some external standard of justice, or that infringes on the rights of third parties.[16] Thus, it is imperative that mediators step up to address such instances of imbalance although doing so is by no means an easy task. Mediators have to first effectively identify where the imbalance lies, and would then have to intervene appropriately, so as to maintain the cooperation and trust of the parties. Nevertheless, mediators should not hide behind the veil of neutrality, and refuse to address the problematic issue of power imbalances. The paper will now move on to discuss how neutrality can in fact be reconciled with the mediator's ability to address imbalances.

III. Reconciling neutrality and power imbalance

A. *Neutrality is not an absolute concept*

The argument that mediator intervention in power imbalances contravenes the notion of neutrality is unconvincing for it fails to recognise the multi-dimensional aspect of neutrality. Discourses on mediator neutrality are often constructed upon an unhelpful binary way of thinking about neutrality as an absolute quality that mediators either do or do not have, rather than viewing it as a complex and constantly fluctuating attribute.[17] A postmodern approach to neutrality would accept these multiple meanings, yet would not insist that each and every one of them is always present or consistently satisfied by a mediator throughout every dispute he or she is called upon to mediate.[18] As such, intervening in instances of power imbalances will only be regarded as a breach of the mediator's neutrality if one seeks to retain absolute concepts of neutrality and power.[19] For instance, Davis and Salem propose that a mediator can compensate for low-level negotiating skills. When a mediator is faced with a party who has minimal negotiating skills, the mediator must take a more active role in helping that party to identify his or her concerns and interest.[20] While this might be perceived as being unequal to one party, the mediator still preserves other aspects of his or her neutrality by being disinterested in the outcome of the dispute.

Another reasoning is that neutrality is not a concept of universal application, but rather, it is a situated concept. Neutrality has several different practical meanings, and is highly dependent on the circumstances of the mediation,[21] as well as the individual parties involved. For mediation services to offer something of value to more people, the mediator must respond to the particulars of the social contexts in which it is offered. Which is to say, the mediator must provide meaningful intervention for all interested parties, addressing the inequalities they experience.[22] Certain situations would warrant the intervention of the mediator more so than in other contexts. In family disputes, mediators exercise a range of neutrality positions during the process, ranging from strict neutrality to an expanded neutrality, depending on the subject of negotiation.[23] This is so as to account for the complexities present in family mediation. Family mediators tend to embrace a stricter neutral stance in relation to the couple's financial or property matters,[24] as it is assumed that both parties are equally competent to negotiate in relation to financial matters. On the other hand, family mediators are regarded as taking a greater intervention-ist role on issues relating to post-separation parenting because such issues often create greater interpersonal conflict for the clients.[25] In the latter example, the mediator will be exercising a more expanded form of neu-trality. The postmodern understanding of neutrality allows for a mediator to legitimately intervene in instances of power imbalances, even if it means having to paradoxically treat the parties unequally, so as to ensure just outcomes between them.[26]

It would be impractical to insist upon a strict compliance with all the meanings of neutrality in every single context. This is probably why crit-ics have proposed that the neutral mediator is a dead one,[27] and that neu-trality is the most pervasive and misleading myth about mediation and is neither a possible attainment nor a desirable one.[28] In certain situations, it might be justified for mediators to adopt a more flexible approach to neu-trality, and for some aspects of a mediator's neutrality to be compromised in ways which would be viewed by many people as entirely acceptable and even necessary.[29] As Astor and Chinkin have noted, mediators have considerable power in mediation and there is evidence that they do not always exercise it in a way which is entirely neutral as to the content and outcome.[30] This has to be the case in order for the mediator to further the greater goals of upholding the moral integrity of the mediation process, by addressing the inequalities that arise.

B. Ensuring fairness in the mediation process

Mediator neutrality and intervening in instances of power imbalance could also be reconciled if one is to take a macroscopic view of "fairness". Fairness should be treated as referring to the mediation process as a whole, and not fairness with respect to the individual parties alone. As stated above, power imbalances have the potential to bring about inequal-ity in the process. The stronger party might use his power to control the mediation process and might even coerce the weaker party into accepting a settlement which is unjust. By failing to intervene on behalf of the party who is being disadvantaged by the mediation process, the mediator can be said to be participating in an unjust and exploitative process.[31] In the *American Bar Association's Standards of Practice for Lawyer Mediators in Family Disputes*, it is specified that part of the mediator's duty to be impartial includes a duty to raise questions as to fairness and equity. Thus, by being sensitive to such imbalances and intervening when necessary, the mediator is actually upholding the fairness of the mediation process.

Furthermore, when the mediation process is strengthened through the enforcement of fair processes, it will in turn help to empower the parties, which is one of the key commitments of the mediator.[32] A mediator can empower the weaker party by assisting the weaker party in obtaining, organising and analysing data, educating the party in planning an effective negotiation strategy and referring the party to a lawyer or other resource person.[33] Sometimes, what a mediator can do is to also help weaker parties identify the power that they already possess. It is important to note that the mediator loses impartiality only when he or she exerts influence in favour of one party at the expense of the other.[34] By empowering the weaker party, the mediator is ensuring that he or she is being placed on a more level playing field to negotiate with the stronger party. The mediator is not, and should not attempt to place restraints on the stronger party. As Davis and Salem have recognised, the mediation process is impartial. By controlling the way in which parties are greeted, seated, addressed, listened to and responded to, it conveys the message that parties are viewed equally.[35] As paradoxical as it sounds, sometimes, it might be necessary to treat parties unequally so as to achieve greater equality in the process.

However, the balancing of powers should be conducted with a caveat in mind. Mediators should only be allowed to bring about fairness in the process, and should not be allowed to alter the substantive outcome. This is because the mediator must be able to provide such support within the context of serving as and being perceived as an impartial third party to the dispute. It may become necessary to explain to the parties that the mediator is not taking a position on the outcome, but rather that he or she is trying to create an equitable negotiation setting so that a settlement can be reached that each party will perceive as reasonable, and therefore be more apt to honour its terms.[36] If a mediator intervenes in the substantive outcome of the dispute, he or she will be overstepping the framework of a mediator's role. This is clearly summarised by Mayer who recognises that the underlying power relations may dictate an unequal result. Mediation, in other words, can provide procedural equality, but cannot usually alter the division of resources or the structural conditions that determine the basic power relations between the parties.[37] Mediators have to remember that they are facilitators of the process, and their role is to help parties arrive at a mutually acceptable decision about issues that are of concern to them.[38] Mediators are not the advocates of the less powerful party, nor the champions of the poor and oppressed.[39] This is echoed in Section 6 of the *UK Law Society's Code of Practice*, which states that power imbalances will almost inevitably exist and will shift during the course of a mediation. The mediator cannot be responsible for redressing those imbalances. He or she must, however, seek to ensure that these do not cause the process to become ineffective as a result of the abuse of one party's stronger position.

Ultimately, the decision to mediate, to continue or to settle must rest with the parties.[40] If the substantive solution still turns out to be one that is grossly unfair, the weaker party has the right to walk away and pursue other means of justice. Section 3.4 of the State Courts of Singapore, *Code of Ethics and Basic Principles on Court Mediation*, states that a mediator shall always respect the parties' right to decide. He shall help the parties clarify the issues, develop and discuss their options but leave the decision on whether and how to settle *solely* with the parties. It is beyond the power of the mediation process to address social ills. However, what the mediator can and should do is to intervene on behalf of the party who is being disadvantaged, so as to help promote the party's self-determination. This is so as to ensure that the inequality that the weaker party faces is not being entrenched further.

IV. The importance of resolving power imbalance

It is important that instances of power imbalances are not being ignored. This is because mediation is gaining established importance as a track to a just result, running parallel with that of the court system. Both have a proper part to play in the administration of justice.[41] If a mediator allows for inequality to propagate through instances of power imbalance, it would be tantamount to going against the notion of justice. This would then jeopardise the role of mediation as an equally appropriate form of dispute resolution. Furthermore, there is also a growing trend of courts encouraging parties to consult mediation as their first stop for dispute resolution.[42] In Singapore, the Supreme Court Practice Directions was amended to introduce the "ADR (Alternative Dispute Resolution) Offer", so as to promote the consideration of ADR at the earliest possible stage. This is to facilitate the just, expeditious and economical disposal of civil cases. Prior to instituting any litigation proceedings, parties would have to submit an ADR form certifying that the lawyers have explained the options and benefits of ADR. With courts actively promoting ADR, it would seem that mediation is expected to provide the same checks and balances as the judicial system does.[43] Thus, it is important for mediators to address such instances of inequality, so as to stress the fairness and justice which the mediation process promises.

V. What is left of neutrality?

Even though the concept of neutrality is one that is hard to understand, it does not mean that the notion of neutrality should be forsaken. This is because neutrality still plays an important legitimising function in mediation.[44] Parties often come to the mediation session under the promise that the mediator will help to resolve the dispute in a neutral manner. The notion of mediator neutrality is further reinforced in the opening statement, where mediators constantly assert that their role in the mediation process is that of a neutral third party, and that he or she will treat parties fairly and without bias. Achieving neutrality is essential if the trust of each party is to be gained and maintained. When gained, a mediator may then confidently use the full range of skills to facilitate a resolution.[45] Furthermore, apart from instilling trust in the parties, the notion that third parties who facilitate or adjudicate disputes must be neutral from the disputants is intrinsically embedded in Western liberal notions of justice.[46] As such, mediator neutrality is important as it is seen as a counterbalance to judicial neutrality, with mediation gaining its legitimacy from its link with the formal judicial system.[47]

However, the current dilemma is that the description of the mediator as "neutral" sets up the parties' expectation of behaviour that may not, cannot, and, maybe, should not be considered as realistic in mediation.[48] This might lead to parties walking away from the mediation because of a perceived breach of neutrality. Perhaps, what mediators can consider doing would be to portray a more realistic picture of what they can do as a neutral third party. Mediators should explain to parties the varying scope of their role as a neutral third party. They should make it clear from the outset that in certain circumstances, there might be a need to intervene to address the imbalances which arise, so as to promote fairness in the process. This pre-empts the parties, and allows them to understand the rationale behind the acts of the mediator. As a result, when mediators do actually intervene in the process, parties will not view this as going against the notion of neutrality. This will ensure that parties continue to trust the mediation process, and will cooperate with the mediator to reach an amicable settlement.

VI. Conclusion

The dichotomy between the mediator's neutrality and the ability to address power imbalances has been widely debated. It is important to see that neutrality is not the nemesis of the mediator's ability to balance powers. As long as the mediator understands what neutrality truly entails, it will become clear that both concepts can exist in a single spectrum, enhancing the role of the mediator as a whole. At the end of the day, the mediator owes a duty to uphold the spirit of mediation as a parallel track to justice. To do so, the mediator must marry both neutrality and the ability to address imbalances, so as to achieve the most desirable outcome for the mediation process.

Endnotes

1. Ruth Charlton & Micheline Dewdney, *The Mediator's Handbook: Skills and Strategies for Practitioners* (Sidney: Lawbook Company, 2nd Edition, 2004) ("*Charlton and Dewdney*") at 292.
2. Laurence Boulle & Teh Hwee Hwee, *Mediation: Principles, Process, Practice* (Singapore: Butterworths Asia, 2000) ("*Boulle*") at 19.
3. *Charlton and Dewdney*, see above note 1 at 291.

4. Hilary Astor, "Mediator Neutrality: Making Sense of Theory and Practice" (2007) 16(2) *Social and Legal Studies* 221 (*"Astor"*) at 223.

5. *Boulle*, see above note 2 at 19.

6. Tony Bogdanoski, "The 'Neutral' Mediator's Perennial Dilemma: To Intervene or not to Intervene?" (2009) 9(1) *Queensland University of Technology Law and Justice Journal* 26 (*"Bogdanoski"*) at 31.

7. Albie M. Davis & Richard A. Salem, "Dealing with Power Imbalances in the Mediation of Interpersonal Disputes" (1984) 6 *Mediation Quarterly* 17 (*"Davis and Salem"*) at 17.

8. *Charlton and Dewdney*, see above note 1 at 309.

9. *Davis and Salem*, see above note 7 at 18.

10. Christopher W. Moore, *The Mediation Process: Practical Strategies for Resolving Conflict* (San Francisco: Jossey-Bass, 2nd Edition, 1996) (*"Moore"*) at 327.

11. Laurence Boulle & Miryana Nesic, *Mediator Skills and Techniques: Triangle of Influence*, (UK: Bloomsbury Professional, 2010) (*"Boulle & Nesic"*) at 265.

12. Hilary Astor & Christine M. Chinkin, *Dispute Resolution in Australia* (London: Butterworths, 1992) (*"Astor & Chinkin"*) at 107.

13. *Astor*, see above note 4 at 236.

14. Rachael Field, "Neutrality and Power: Myths and Reality" (2000) 3(1) *ADR Bulletin* 16 at 18.

15. *Astor & Chinkin*, see above note 12 at p 152.

16. David Greatbatch & Robert Dingwall, "Selective Facilitation: Some Observations on a Strategy Used by Divorce Mediators" (1989) 23(4) *Law and Society Review* 613 at 614.

17. *Bogdanoski*, see above note 6 at 39.

18. *Bogdanoski*, see above note 6 at 39.

19. *Bogdanoski*, see above note 6 at 27.

20. *Davis and Salem*, see above note 7 at 20.

21. *Astor & Chinkin*, see above note 12 at 153.

22. Leah Wing, "Mediation and Inequality Reconsidered: Bringing the Discussion to the Table" (2009) *Conflict Resolution Quarterly* 383 at p 391.

23. Alison Taylor, "Concepts of Neutrality in Family Mediation: Contexts, Ethics, Influence, and Transformative Process" (1997) 14(3) Mediation Quarterly 215 (*"Taylor"*) at 226–227.

24. *Taylor*, see above note 23 at 227.

25. *Taylor*, see above note 23 at 227.

26. *Bogdanoski*, see above note 6 at 27–28.

27. Greg Tillett, Domestic Violence and Mediation Conference (Sydney, 26 October 1991).

28. *Boulle*, see above note 2 at 19.

29. *Astor & Chinkin*, see above note 12 at 105.

30. *Astor & Chinkin*, see above note 12 at 102.

31. *Astor & Chinkin*, see above note 12 at 163.

32. Bernard Mayer, "The Dynamics of Power in Mediation and Negotiation" (1987) 16 *Mediation Quarterly* 75 ("*Mayer*") at 81.

33. *Moore*, see above note 10 at 337.

34. *Mayer*, see above note 32 at 83.

35. *Davis and Salem*, see above note 7 at 19.

36. *Davis and Salem*, see above note 7 at 19.

37. *Mayer*, see above note 33 at 81–82.

38. *Mayer*, see above note 33 at 83.

39. *Boulle & Nesic*, see above note 11 at 264.

40. *Charlton and Dewdney*, see above note 1 at 312.

41. As per Lord Justice Ward in *Burchell v Bullard* [2005] EWCA (Civ) 358 at [43].

42. As per Lord Justice Dyson in *Halsey v Milton Keynes NHS Trust and Steel v Joy and Halliday* [2004] EWCA (Civ) 576 at [11]. Note also former Chief Justice Chan Sek Keong's keynote address in the October 2012 ADR Conference at [19].

43. *Bogdanoski*, see above note 6 at 35.

44. *Boulle*, see above note 2 at 19.

45. *Charlton and Dewdney*, see above note 1 at 294.

46. *Astor*, see above note 4 at 236–237.

47. *Boulle*, see above note 2 at p 30.

48. Rober D Benjamin, "The Risk of Neutrality — Reconsidering the Term and Concept" (1998) 17(3) *Ethics Forum, Mediation News* 8 at 8–9.